ROUTLEDGE LIBRARY EDITIONS: REVOLUTION IN ENGLAND

Volume 2

ALLEGIANCE IN CHURCH AND STATE

ALLEGIANCE IN CHURCH AND STATE

The Problem of the Nonjurors in the English Revolution

L. M. HAWKINS

LONDON AND NEW YORK

First published in 1928 by George Routledge & Sons, Ltd.

This edition first published in 2023
by Routledge
4 Park Square, Milton Park, Abingdon, Oxon OX14 4RN

and by Routledge
605 Third Avenue, New York, NY 10158

Routledge is an imprint of the Taylor & Francis Group, an informa business

© 1928

All rights reserved. No part of this book may be reprinted or reproduced or utilised in any form or by any electronic, mechanical, or other means, now known or hereafter invented, including photocopying and recording, or in any information storage or retrieval system, without permission in writing from the publishers.

Trademark notice: Product or corporate names may be trademarks or registered trademarks, and are used only for identification and explanation without intent to infringe.

British Library Cataloguing in Publication Data
A catalogue record for this book is available from the British Library

ISBN: 978-1-032-47827-2 (Set)
ISBN: 978-1-032-47235-5 (Volume 2) (hbk)
ISBN: 978-1-032-47239-3 (Volume 2) (pbk)
ISBN: 978-1-003-38518-9 (Volume 2) (ebk)

DOI: 10.4324/9781003385189

Publisher's Note
The publisher has gone to great lengths to ensure the quality of this reprint but points out that some imperfections in the original copies may be apparent.

Disclaimer
The publisher has made every effort to trace copyright holders and would welcome correspondence from those they have been unable to trace.

ALLEGIANCE IN CHURCH AND STATE

The Problem of the Nonjurors
in the English Revolution

By

L. M. HAWKINS

With a Foreword by

G. P. GOOCH
D.Litt., F.B.A.

LONDON
GEORGE ROUTLEDGE & SONS, LTD.
BROADWAY HOUSE: 68-74, CARTER LANE, E.C.
1928

*Thesis approved for the Degree of Doctor
of Philosophy in the University of London*

Printed in Great Britain by
MACKAYS LTD., CHATHAM

CONTENTS

	PAGE
FOREWORD BY DR. G. P. GOOCH	vii

CHAPTER

I THE BACKGROUND
1. Early Seventeenth-Century Theories of Divine Right ... 1
2. The Middle of the Century ... 17
3. After the Restoration ... 24

II THE NONJURING CHURCH
1. James II. and the Anglican Church ... 34
2. The "State Point." ... 40
3. The "Church Point." ... 47

III THE ORIGIN AND AIMS OF MONARCHICAL GOVERNMENT
1. Monarchy ... 56
2. The Succession ... 57
3. The End of Government ... 60
4. The Origin of Society and Government ... 63
5. The Case Against the Contract ... 66

IV SOVEREIGNTY
1. Source and Nature of Authority ... 77
2. Authority and Law ... 88
3. Authority and the Subject ... 92

CONTENTS

CHAPTER		PAGE
V	CHURCH AND STATE	
	1. Distinction between Permanent and Occasional Aspects of the Problem	105
	2. The Oaths	107
	3. Schism and Immoral Prayers	111
	4. Religion as a Power in the State	118
	5. Inalienability of Spiritual Power	122
	6. The Church as a Spiritual Society	124
VI	CHARLES LESLIE	
	1. Controversialist and Nonjuror	131
	2. Theory of State Sovereignty	133
	3. The Sovereignty of the Church	149
VII	LATER DEVELOPMENTS OF ANGLO-CATHOLIC POLITICAL THEORY	
	1. The Doctrine of Divine Right	160
	2. The Political Issue	162
	3. The Relationship of Church and State	168
BIBLIOGRAPHY		193
INDEX		197

FOREWORD

THERE is no more fruitful or fascinating portion of the vast field of historical studies than the evolution of ideas and ideals, their relation to political and economic events, and their influence on the lives of their friends and foes. A particularly rich quarry is provided by Seventeenth-Century England, which witnessed the beginning of both the constitutional and the intellectual transition from the old order to the new. We are an argumentative race, and our habit of stating reasons for what we do has given birth to political classics which are known throughout the world. If, however, we are fully to understand the mind and character of modern society, we must not confine our attention to the giant thinkers and the victorious side, but must hearken also to the pleading of lesser men and recapture the outlook of warriors who have gone down in the fight.

The present volume is a singularly thoughtful, suggestive and well-balanced essay in the art of historical interpretation. Miss Hawkins has chosen a theme of real interest and importance, which has been unduly neglected. Though the Nonjurors are universally respected for their piety, learning and fidelity to conscience, their political ideas have seemed too preposterous to deserve detailed analysis. It is her achievement to render them intelligible and to emphasize the valuable elements in their creed, without being in the least convinced by their arguments, or indulging in sentimental regrets at the extinction of their sect. A generation ago Figgis explained the doctrine of Divine Right as an expression of the sound instinct for strong government ; and Miss Hawkins, continuing the story which he began, exhibits Nonjurors as witnesses to the need of moral foundations for a State and the sacredness of moral obligations in public life. In the writings clearly and concisely analysed in these pages we may read once again that all authority derives from God ; that power is one and indivisible ; that His sole repository is the legitimate King ; that the only alternative to autocracy is mob rule ; and that it is better to obey an unworthy ruler than to expose the community to the horrors of civil war.

There was nothing new in the pamphlets of that brilliant gladiator, Charles Leslie, and his comrades ; for, as Miss Hawkins points out, the task of the Nonjurors of 1689 was less to create a case than to sustain a tradition. But though the arguments were in essence those of James I. and Filmer, the atmosphere had changed, and the conduct of James II. made it impossible for the average man and even for the average Churchman to swallow the Gospel of Divine Right. The King's ill-judged attack on the Church, hitherto the chief support of the Crown, compelled Church people to look with more critical eyes at the Royal Prerogative itself. Moreover, the Nation as a whole declined to believe that the only choice was between tyranny and anarchy ; and accepting the assurance of Locke that a mixed government was both possible and desirable, proceeded with the leisurely construction of our constitutional liberties. The Revolution Settlement was the triumph of common sense. The last of the Die-hards were brushed aside because the modern Englishman is practical, prosaic, and empirical, inclined to compromise, caring nothing for mysticism and little for logic, but testing the value of institutions and principles by their fruits alone.

G. P. Gooch.

ALLEGIANCE IN CHURCH AND STATE

THE PROBLEM OF THE NONJURORS IN THE ENGLISH REVOLUTION

CHAPTER I

THE BACKGROUND

1. *Early Seventeenth-Century Theories of Divine Right.*

THE elimination of Spain as an actively hostile Catholic power had left the Church *in* England free to effect its own establishment as the Church *of* England. The Anglican Church, which as a young cutting had been pruned from the Roman stock had, in its sapling stage, been nourished with the blood of the Marian martyrs, and had thriven in the sunny prosperity of the last of the Tudors. The Stuart kings arrived upon the English scene in time to find the sturdy tree fruiting, with new growths and fresh forms springing up around it. Politically these offshoots of Anglicanism became manifest in the struggle for a free and sovereign Parliament; ecclesiastically they grew and multiplied in the numberless conventicles of the sects scattered throughout the length and breadth of England.

James I., a foreigner, the son of Catholic Mary, the King of Calvinist Scotland, and a man who combined extreme views on the dignity of the kingly office with extreme lack of dignity in his kingly person, might have found his position in England somewhat precarious had he not early endeared himself to the Anglican Church by his avowed abhorrence of both Rome and Geneva. But it was characteristic of the early Stuarts to see in the claims of supremacy still made by the Roman Church an unwarrantable and exorbitant encroachment by an alien institution upon the sovereignty of an independent National King. They regarded the parallel claims for autonomy in Church and State made by the Puritans and Presbyterians as nothing short of blasphemous. The Anglican Church was a Heaven-born refuge, alike from the imperiousness of an older generation and the impudence of a younger. It was their great good fortune that in England they found a National Church on which they could thus count for loyal support.

The admiration and confidence were moreover mutual. The bishops were equally in need of a defence from the arrogance of foreign interference, and the demands for reform and more democratic control at home. An alliance with the throne was seen to be the only safeguard against both "new presbyter" and "old priest." The theory of the Divine Right of Kings, which had early shown the way to a new focus for the allegiances shattered by the revolt from the Papacy, provided a doctrinal rallying point for both King and Church. Thus the sovereignty of the Pope and the supremacy of the Roman Church gave way before the sovereignty of the King and the authority of the Anglican Church; the laws of the King in Parliament superseded Papal Bulls in the ordering of ecclesiastical affairs; Divine Right, which was obviously no longer inherent in the Pope, was discovered to be inseparable from the King; infallibility, no longer presumed to be an attribute of the Bishop of Rome, must be found in the Scriptures; passive obedience, no longer due to the Romish hierarchy, was owing to the English throne.

The first Stuart occupant of the throne, not renowned as a swordsman, wielded a pen with no little distinction. His works were in the van of that massed array whereby seventeenth-century Anglicans sought to justify their dual allegiance to Church and State. At a later date the English Nonjurors were gallantly to fight the rear-guard action in defence of the same position with weapons but slightly dissimilar from those of the earlier generation. But inasmuch as they looked backwards and not forwards, they failed to see that the doctrine of Divine Right had accomplished its end and was no longer worth their defence.

James I. issued an edition of the *Basilikon Doron* in England within a few months of his accession. This work displayed streaks of almost startling modernism side by side with observations redolent of mediæval superstition. In it the King urged his son to use all other princes as brethren, and always to delay as long as possible before taking up the sword in war, but immediately followed this twentieth-century-sounding advice with warnings of portentous seriousness against the practice of consulting necromancers and soothsayers. The simple sincerity of the King's exhortations on the religious obligations of kingship was matched in the second part of the book with many sound observations on affairs financial, legal, military and administrative. The King's political creed was further expounded in *The True Law of Free Monarchies*, published in the same year, in which an attempt was made to answer objections to his dogmas and to emphasize the reciprocal nature of the bond between " a free king and his natural subjects." The avowed object of this second treatise was to persuade Christian subjects not to rebel.

The most definite and concise statement concerning the divine nature of monarchy made by King James, appeared in a revised edition of Part II of *Basilikon Doron*, issued, significantly enough, at a time when his son's difficulties were becoming most acute in 1642, under the title *The Duty of a King in His Royal Office*. Here it was declared that "the state of monarchy is the supremest thing upon earth, for Kings are not only God's lieutenants upon earth, and sit upon God's throne, but even by God himself they are called Gods. . . . God hath power to create or destroy, make or unmake at his pleasure, to give life, or send death, to judge all, and to be judged nor accomptable to none; to raise low things, and to make high things low at his pleasure, and to God are both soul and body due. And the like power have kings."[1] " Monarchy as a form of govern-

[1] *The Duty of a King in His Royal Office*, 1642.

ment, resembling the Divinity, approacheth nearest to perfection . . . unity being the perfection of all things."[1] It seems somewhat unfortunate for the advocates of this view of monarchy that a king, being *ipso facto* a "little God," does not necessarily acquire the moral character of the Deity at the same moment as he inherits the divine prerogative. James included in his *Advice To His Dearest Son Henry*, a carefully-drawn distinction between a good king and a tyrant, and their respective methods of government, and added a multitude of moral maxims designed to assist the development of virtue in the Prince. The king should be an example of virtue to all his subjects as a father to his children, "for by the law of nature a king becomes the natural father to all his lieges at his coronation."[2] But although this Coronation Oath was "the clearest civil and fundamental law whereby the king's office is properly defined,"[3] the relationship which it confirmed was a relationship between God and the king, rather than between the king and his people, for the king, though giving a promise to rule by law and to protect his subjects, was not accountable to them if he broke it, but to God who alone may judge him, being the sole source of his authority and power.

It was inevitable that the grounds of his accession to the English throne should lead James to examine the origins of monarchy, but while formally tracing them to Jewish history, he acknowledged that in

---

[1] *The True Law of Free Monarchies*, 1603.
[2] *Ibid.*   [3] *Ibid.*

England the institution arose out of conquest, and not from any kind of law or contract framed by the people. He also formulated the *Rex non moritur* doctrine, which played such an important part in the later history of the House of Stuart. The king is the "heritable overlord, and so by birth, not by any right in the coronation, cometh to his crown . . . for at the moment of the expiring of the king reigning the nearest and lawful heir entereth in his place, and so to refuse him or intrude another is not to hold out one coming in, but to expel and put out their righteous king."[1] A more apt and illuminating statement of the Nonjuring view in 1688–9 would be difficult to find.

The insistence on the divine nature of monarchy led on inevitably to an equally ardent advocacy of passive obedience and non-resistance. "As to dispute what God may do is blasphemy . . . so it is sedition in subjects to dispute what a king may do in the height of his power."[2] God, who alone has power to make kings, is likewise the sole authority who may unmake them. James illustrated the subject's lack of power from the Old Testament incident of the Jews demanding a king, and pictured Samuel thus addressing the Jews. "It is not only the ordinance of God, but also yourselves have chosen him unto you, thereby renouncing for ever all privileges by your willing consent out of your hands, whereby in any time thereafter ye would claim and call back unto yourselves again that power,

---

[1] *The True Law of Free Monarchies.*
[2] *The Duty of a King in His Royal Office.*

which God shall not permit you to do."[1] God did not allow even his chosen people to resist tyrants, much less will he permit any others to claim the right. Their obedience was due to their king " as to God's Lieutenant in Earth . . . following and obeying his lawful commands, eschewing and flying his fury in his unlawful without resistance but by sobs and tears to God."[2] Even if, as many presumed, contract were implied in the Coronation Oath, yet the default of one party thereto could not justify rebellion on the side of the other, for a man cannot be judge in his own case, and " since God is the only judge between two parties' contractors, the cognition and revenge must only appertain to him."[3] Further, the king was said to be the father of his people, and the head of the Church, and was thus on a plane where resistance, besides being immoral, would run counter to all known laws of nature. Nor could rebellion even justify itself in the issue, but only add misery to misery, for no king, not even a tyrant, must be judged as wholly bad, and success in conflict does not necessarily prove the righteousness of the cause. A wicked king should be regarded as a just chastisement sent by God to avenge the sins of the people; repentance and endurance were attitudes meet for such a visitation rather than judgment or resistance.

In the early years of the seventeenth century the position of a National Church, with less than a hundred years of independent history, was still

---
[1] *The True Law of Free Monarchies.*
[2] *Ibid.*   [3] *Ibid.*

8 ALLEGIANCE IN CHURCH AND STATE

deemed too precarious to allow thoughts of toleration. The Pope was hated, but the Anglican Church had not yet broken from the age-long Catholic tradition sufficiently to despise or ignore him. In 1605, the smouldering animosity with which Englishmen regarded Rome was fanned to a blaze by news of the Gunpowder Plot. The Government followed up its summary and barbarous treatment of the conspirators by the publication of the Oath of Allegiance, which contained an even more emphatic denunciation of Papal claims to universal obedience than had been expressed in the original Oath of Supremacy on the King's accession. It was intended to serve as a test to distinguish those who were Catholics first and Englishmen after, (*i.e.*, those who refused to own James rather than the Pope as sovereign) from those who were first and foremost loyal subjects of the Crown. The Pope condemned the Oath and warned the Catholics that they could only take it at the risk of eternal damnation. Cardinal Bellarmine was one of the most distinguished of those who wrote against its imposition. In 1609, James published, in reply to Bellarmine, an apology prefaced by " a premonition . . . to all most mighty monarchs, kings and free princes," in which he explained the circumstances in which the Oath had been framed. " The Lower House of Parliament at the first framing of this Oath made it contain that the Pope had no power to excommunicate me, which I caused them to reform, only making it conclude that no excommunication of the Pope's can warrant my subjects to practise against my person or State, denying the deposition of kings to be in the Pope's lawful power." "Laics as well as Churchmen are subject to none but their natural sovereign."[1] Hence the Pope's condemnation of the Oath was void, nor could he claim any obedience which would run counter to the relationship of loyalty between king and subject.

The beginnings of the long dispute between Crown and Parliament, which was ultimately to occasion the eclipse, not only of the Stuarts, but also of the doctrine of Divine Right, were likewise reflected in the writings of James. The obedience which he claimed as due to his person representing God on earth, was due equally to the expression of his will through law. "The kings were the authors and makers of laws, not the laws of the kings,"[2] and hence the royal will was the final source of political authority. He did, indeed, go so far as to acknowledge that " Parliament has been ordained for making laws,"[3] but this "making" was to be interpreted as signifying nothing more than a right of request, "for, albeit the king make daily statutes and ordinances . . . without any advice of Parliament or Estates, yet it lies in the power of no Parliament to make any kind of law or statute without his sceptre be put to it for giving it the force of law."[4] As a corollary to this doctrine he asserted that "general laws made publicly in Parliament may upon known respects to the king by his authority be mitigated and suspended on causes only known

---

[1] *An Apology for the Oath of Allegiance*, 1609.
[2] *The True Law of Free Monarchies*.
[3] *Basilikon Doron*, Part II.
[4] *The True Law of Free Monarchies.*

to him."[1] The application of this theory by his two grandsons was among the sharpest controversial weapons of the later seventeenth century. James I., who had not the triumphs of the Long Parliament as his political background, not only claimed dispensing power over the laws, but avowed his belief in the desirability of dispensing as far as possible with Parliament itself. " Hold no Parliaments but for necessity of new laws, which would be but seldom, for few laws and well put into execution are best in a well-ruled Commonwealth," and " in this country we have already more good laws than are well executed."[2]

The political arguments used by James were repeated in varying dress and with varying emphasis by many writers before the year 1640. The pamphlet entitled *God and the King*, reputed to be by Richard Mocket, an Anglican divine who was Warden of All Souls', Oxford, was in dialogue form. In it the Oath of Allegiance was upheld by one speaker in face of the criticisms expressed and questions asked by the other. It was first published in 1615 "by his Majesty's special privilege and command," and ran through several editions, achieving under the influence of its royal sponsor a vast circulation in both kingdoms. This discussion traced the grounds of sovereignty to English law as well as to God's ordinance, and quoted extensively from Bracton. Its condemnation of resistance, as contrary both to the law of Nature and the moral

---

[1] *The True Law of Free Monarchies.*
[2] *Basilikon Doron*, Part II.

THE BACKGROUND

law, was phrased in exaggerated terms—not even in defence of Christianity itself was resistance to be allowed.

Moreover, the King found among the lawyers some who supported his doctrine with no less fervency than did the clergy, though the legal profession was not by any means unanimous in its political allegiance. In the celebrated case of John Bate in 1606, when the Barons of the Exchequer upheld the Crown against the petition of the Commons, another aspect of the century's constitutional struggle was initiated. To the House, which was endeavouring to achieve the right to control finance, Chief Baron Fleming returned answer that the King's prerogative was to be respected in all cases. "The wisdom and providence of the king is not to be disputed by the subject; for by intendment they cannot be severed from his person, and to argue *a posse ad actum* to restrain the king and his power because that by his power he may do ill, is no argument for a subject."[1] The question of Impositions was not to be settled in this fashion, however, and it remained as a source of contention until the days of the Long Parliament.

The House of Commons was as eager to maintain its own rights as the King to preserve his, and resolutely protested against the views on the royal prerogative expressed by Dr. Cowell, Professor of Civil Law at Cambridge. In his book, *The Interpreter*, which he dedicated to the Archbishop of Canterbury, this academic lawyer asserted that the king is

[1] Quoted in Prothero's *Statutes and Constitutional Documents*, fourth edition.

"above the law by his absolute power, and though for the better and equal course in making laws he do admit the three estates . . . unto council, yet this, in divers learned men's opinions, is not of constraint but of his own benignity, or by reason of his promise made upon oath at the time of his coronation. For otherwise were he a subject after a sort, and subordinate, which may not be thought without breach of duty and loyalty . . . and though at his coronation he take an oath not to alter the laws of the land, yet, this oath notwithstanding, he may alter or suspend any particular law that seemeth hurtful to the public estate." James, being in grave financial difficulty at the time, was compelled to placate the House by joining in the outcry against this insult to its dignity, but it is significant that *The Interpreter*, after being publicly burned in 1610, was re-issued no less than three times before 1689, and finally reached a sixth edition in the time of the second George.

William Laud, who was destined later, as Archbishop of Canterbury, to personify the quintessence of English Arminianism, had already, during the reign of James I., formulated a much more positive theory of the relationship of Church and State than was to be found in the King's denunciatory outbursts against Puritan and Papist. "Both Commonwealth and Church are collective bodies, made up of many into one. And both so near allied that the one, the Church, can never subsist but in the other, the Commonwealth. Nay, so near, that the same men which in a temporal respect make the Commonwealth

THE BACKGROUND

do in a spiritual make the Church. The Commonwealth can have no blessed and happy being but by the Church. For true religion ever blesses a State."[1] He solemnly warned the nation of the danger afforded to the State by the existence of division within the Church, and stressed again and again the mutual dependence of the one upon the other. " These three, God, the King, and the Church, that is, God, his Spouse and his Lieutenant upon Earth, are so near allied . . . that no man can serve any one of them truly but he serves all three."[2] This man, who was preaching at a time when each week saw new conventicles added to the old, and when the growing restiveness of Parliament was matched by the growing fanaticism of the Puritans, was determined to go to any length in order to preserve unity in Church and State. The lengths to which he afterwards went in the case of Prynne, to name but one example, prove that in his passion for unity he was at least sincere. That his sincerity so effectually obliterated his charity was a misfortune, partly the result and partly the cause of the struggles of his day. Just as the notion that sovereignty was divisible or resistance allowable was inconceivable to any Anglican politician of that age, so was it impossible for Laud to admit that the Church might acknowledge the rights of the separatists to independence either in worship or thought. He condemned parity in the Church, as

[1] Sermon preached before his Majesty, 19th June, 1621.
[2] Sermon preached at the opening of Parliament, 6th February, 1625.

being incompatible with the safety of Monarchy, and thus as endangering the State itself, for the factions of aristocracy and the turbulence of democracy were alike inimical to the stability of government. The rule of one in the Church was as essential to peace as the rule of one in the State.

This assumption of the identity of Church and State reappeared in the sermon on "Apostolic Obedience," by Robert Sybthorpe. He asserted that the excellency of the relationship between the two in England lay in the fact that they were in truth but one institution, being composed of the same members, differentiated only in relation to spiritual or civil ends. That is, the difference was purely one of function rather than of constitution. This situation was shown to be in marked contrast to that existing in France and Scotland, " the one of which makes the Church above the king and the Pope above the Church, and so dethrones Princes by his thunderbolts of excommunications and deprivation. The other makes the law above the king and the people above the law, and so depose Princes by their tumult and insurrections."[1] The reference to France was apt, in view of King Charles' Catholic marriage, and the dilemma in which his endeavours to please Louis by the promise of relief for Catholics in this country, while seeking to please English Protestants by schemes for assisting the Huguenots in France, had placed him. It was doubtless due to Sybthorpe's eloquent appeal that his hearers should

[1] Sermon on *Apostolic Obedience* preached at the Northampton Assizes, February 22nd, 1626.

"render to all their dues," coming as it did at a time when the country was being pressed for a loan by Charles, that the sermon was so well received in the royal favour. The King swept aside all objections which the Archbishop of Canterbury and others raised against it, and insisted on its being licensed for publication. The author, however, while expressing the extremest form of the doctrine of non-resistance, was far removed from that worship of monarchy which regarded the King as a God, and therefore incapable of wrong. The Prince, he said, "doth whatsoever pleaseth him, and where the word of the King is, there is power,"[1] but obedience was due, not because the will of the ruler was coincident with the divine will, for a prince was as open to error as any man, but solely because resistance would imperil the soul. For the sake of credit, policy, duty or conscience, obedience was best; where active obedience was found to be physically or morally impossible, it was to give way to unquestioning passive obedience (accompanied still by prayerful fidelity), even if such procedure involved for the subject the utmost rigours of punishment.

The case of Roger Maynwaring, a royal chaplain, was an illuminating reflection of the political controversy of his time. In two sermons on "Religion and Allegiance," preached before the King in 1627, Maynwaring, with considerable eloquence, set forth the claims of the Royal prerogative then current as sound doctrine in the Anglican Church. Among other things he asserted that "lawful

[1] *Apostolic Obedience.*

sovereigns are no less than Fathers, Lords, Kings and Gods on earth,"[1] lower only in the hierarchy of all created beings than God himself, that even God stands " in the assembly of Princes as one of them,"[2] and " no power in the world [or] in the hierarchy of the Church can lay restraint upon these supremes,"[3] for the power of kings " is not merely human, but superhuman, and indeed no less than a Power Divine,"[4] and that " Justice intercedes not between God and men, not between the Prince being a Father and the People as children (for Justice is between equals)."[5] To Maynwaring, this perfect embodiment of religious conservatism, one main function of the Church was to inculcate a wholesale and unquestioning obedience in subjects towards the royal authority, not as a matter of precedent or expedience, but as a vital necessity for the salvation of those souls entrusted to its care. " No subject," he declared, " may, without hazard of his own damnation in rebelling against God, question or disobey the will and pleasure of his sovereign."[6] While acknowledging Assemblies in the State as " sacred, honourable and necessary," he yet declared that they were not ordained " to contribute any right to kings . . . but for the more equal imposing and more easy exacting of that, which, unto kings doth appertain by natural and original law and justice; as their proper inheritance annexed to their imperial crowns

[1] Sermon at Oatlands, 4th July, 1627.
[2] Sermon at Alderton, 29th July, 1627.
[3] Sermon at Oatlands. [4] *Ibid.*
[5] Sermon at Alderton.
[6] Sermon at Oatlands.

THE BACKGROUND

from their very births."[1] Archbishop Abbot took up the same position in Maynwaring's case as he had done in that of Sybthorpe, and refused to grant a license for publication. Even Laud demurred on the ground that the people would find this doctrine very distasteful; but Charles overbore all objections, and persuaded Montaigne, then Bishop of London, to stand sponsor to the sermons, though this prelate afterwards confessed to the House of Lords that he had not himself read them. The House of Commons not unnaturally resented the publication of this flagrant attack on its status and privilege, and condemned the preacher to lengthy imprisonment, the payment of a heavy fine, and the suspension from all ecclesiastical office. The King was temporarily forced to bow before the storm, and issued a proclamation for the suppression of the book; but an early grant of pardon, followed by the gift of more than one new benefice, and subsequently of the Bishopric of St. Davids, indicated his true regard for his Chaplain. The two Parliaments of 1640 successively returned to the assault at a time when Charles was no longer strong enough to mitigate the severity of their attack, and Maynwaring was finally deprived of office on account both of his extreme doctrine and suspected Romish practices.

2. *The Middle of the Century.*

Simultaneously with his contemptuous dealings with the English Parliament, the King was becoming

[1] Sermon at Oatlands

involved in controversy with his Scottish subjects over the attempted introduction of Anglican ecclesiastical forms in the Presbyterian Church. In accordance with his cherished plan of establishing the Anglican Church in a safe position, midway between the traditional domination of Rome and the upstart enthusiasm of the Sects, James had effected the nominal restoration of Episcopacy in Scotland as a bulwark against the Presbyterian order dear to Scottish Calvinists. Charles, to complete his father's work, attempted to force upon an unwilling Church, still Presbyterian in everything but name, the English Liturgy. Hence he added the exasperation of his Northern subjects to the growing unpopularity created in the South by his Catholic marriage, his financial policy, his unconstitutional courts, his favourites, and his policy of personal government. The increasing strength of the King's party, even after Strafford and Laud had paid the final penalty, is proof in itself of the intensity of current belief in the doctrine of Divine Right. Indeed, by an inevitable process of reaction, the defeat, trial and execution of Charles proved to be a magnificent piece of propaganda for the Royalist and Anglican cause. The Parliament, though it had ostensibly fought in the name of the King's authority, and achieved success against the King's person, failed to bring in the millennium in its efforts to exercise the King's sovereignty. The shifting of power from Crown to Parliament and from the Bishops to the Westminster Assembly, was too sudden and complete, and the attempt to establish a new equilibrium failed. Once the star of Oliver Cromwell was in the ascendant, the real rule of the country passed to the army, and thereafter the Parliament was the tool or toy of the military forces, to be purged, expelled, recalled or dissolved as the occasion demanded. But a military dictatorship only served to hasten the reaction. The " Humble Petition and Advice," presented in 1656, showed how deep-rooted was the habit of loyalty to the Crown. Many influential men, both in and out of the House of Commons, believed in the institution of monarchy with far greater fervour than they believed in the family of Stuart, and recognizing Cromwell's ability as a statesman, would fain have been subject to His Majesty King Oliver rather than to His Highness the Lord Protector Cromwell. They assumed that, if kingship were in truth a divine institution, then God would graciously confer on the House of Commons that right which the House of Stuart had so obviously forfeited.

By a strange irony, the Restoration of monarchy was effected through an alliance of Presbyterians with Anglican royalists—these incongruous partners being thrown together in an endeavour to escape from the mild mediocrity of Richard Cromwell on the one hand, and the republican fanaticism of the army on the other.

Although in the long processes of history a temporary eclipse of eleven years may leave but little mark on the surface of political institutions, it is inevitable that the concepts underlying them and the formulæ by which they are supported must undergo considerable modification, if not complete change, by the very existence of such historical facts as regicide and revolution. Hence, while 1660 saw the Restoration not only of the monarchy but also of the House of Stuart, and the crumpling up of the political radicalism espoused by the sects, thenceforward affairs are seen from a new angle, and the discussion of politics is, by a majority of writers, carried on on a new basis.

Allowance must, of course, be made for the host of flatterers seeking by fulsome adulation to ensure for themselves the certainty of royal favour at a time when suspicion was rife. Moreover, apart from the doubtful sincerity of some of the more extravagant expressions of loyalty to the Crown and Church, there may be heard tones of genuine jubilation at the vindication of the Royal cause and the triumphant resurrection of Anglicanism. The common downfall of Republicans and Presbyterians was truly a matter for deep thankfulness on the part of hundreds who quite sincerely believed that the constitution of pre-1640 England was the true and final expression of the will of the divine Ruler of the Universe, and the only safe stronghold against the sinful designs of Roman Catholics and separatists alike.

But when the glib and genial Vicars of Bray have been set aside, and a discount made for the natural self-congratulations of the Erastians, even a cursory examination of the residue of the political writings of the Restoration period reveals the emergence of a subtly different attitude of mind in the writers, in part engendered by the nature of recent and current events, and in part the outcrop in the English mind

THE BACKGROUND

of a general movement towards the secularization of political thought.

In an earlier age the common acceptance of the Scriptures as verbally inspired and historically accurate, together with the low standard of literary education among the peasant class, had made it easy for Catholic divines to impose upon their flocks that interpretation of the Bible which best suited the Roman system and doctrine. In its beginnings the Reformation in England had been conditioned almost entirely by political considerations. Coming as it did by way of Lutheranism, it left the Church still the seat of authority and the guardian of individual consciences. It was not until the Bible was an open book and the common possession of people through the length and breadth of the land, that the Reformation really became a matter for intellectual acceptance rather than for passionate patriotism. Unfortunately, by that time the Anglican Church had had time to become hardened in form and crystallized in doctrine. Force of circumstances made it act on the defensive in the sixteenth century, and by the seventeenth the attitude of defence was habitual, precluding it from the possibility of enlarging its borders or of seeking peace with those whom it believed to be its enemies.

But these enemies had taken much of their inspiration and power from the self-same source as that which the parent Church had drawn upon for so long. If Cromwell's psalm-singing soldiers of the New Model, Winstanley's Agrarian Communists, Lilburne's Levellers, and the multitudinous fanatical sects all based their outrageous defiance of the Constitution on their study of the Word of God, were the protagonists of the Divine Right of Kings altogether on safe ground in relying solely on the Book themselves ? Royalist controversialists became inoculated with doubt, and the efficacy of text-flinging as a form of argument was called in question. This movement towards the secularization of political thought was strengthened by contact with Continental philosophy and science during the exile of the Court. Thus, after the Restoration of the monarchy the conception of Natural Rights occupies a position of continually increasing importance. Theocratic doctrines tend to fall into the background, while prominence is given to rationalistic theories built upon the twin foundations of historical and utilitarian arguments. The discussion of Government grows more abstract, and while the theory of law receives far more attention than before, much less is said about the sacredness of the king's person and the religious duty of passive obedience.

"It is a shame and scandal," wrote Sir Robert Filmer in 1648, "for us Christians to seek the original of government from the inventions or fictions of poets, orators, philosophers and heathen historians who all lived thousands of years after the Creation, and were (in a manner) ignorant of it ; and to neglect the Scriptures which have with more authority most particularly given us the true grounds and Principles of Government."[1] But thirty years later it was in no way remarkable for the author of *Christian*

[1] *The Anarchy of a Limited or Mixed Monarchy.*

Loyalty, an Anglican divine, to assert that " the rights of Christian Princes do not directly depend upon the political constitution of the Jews, or the family of Jacob, but are founded in the laws of Nature, of nations and of Christianity," and " that Government and its authority is originally the constitution of God, may receive considerable proof from rational evidence."[1]

Thus, while some of the arguments from Old Testament and early Church History persist long after 1660, more especially in the political sermons with which it was the custom to celebrate the anniversaries of January 30th and May 29th, there was a growing tendency to supplement such data by an appeal to reason and abstract conceptions of law and sovereignty. Dr. Robert South, Public Orator of the University of Oxford, and Chaplain to the Lord High Chancellor, preaching at Lambeth in 1666, declared that " our religion is a religion that dares to be understood ; that offers itself to the search of the inquisitive, to the inspection of the severest and most awakened reason . . . it needs no legends . . . no altering or bribing the voice of antiquity to speak for it ; it needs none of all those laborious artifices of ignorance ; none of all these cloaks and coverings."[2] This valiant claim was followed up by the assertion that " the Church of England glories in nothing more than she is the truest friend to kings, and to kingly government, of any other Church in the world ;

---

[1] *Christian Loyalty*, by William Falkner, London, 1679.
[2] A Sermon preached at Lambeth Chapel upon the consecration of the Lord Bishop of Rochester, November 25th, 1666.

that they were the same hands and principles that took the crown from the king's head and the mitre from the Bishops."

3. *After the Restoration.*

A Church in such a state of mind was in the mood neither for compromise nor for toleration. The Government party in the 1660 Convention had had no sympathy with Charles' soothing promises of "liberty to tender consciences" made in the Declaration of Breda, and the discussions on the scheme for comprehension, upon which the Presbyterians had based their hope of retaining power, were fruitless. The failure of the Convention to arrive at any ecclesiastical settlement was soon remedied by its successor. The Cavalier Parliament of 1661 was overwhelmingly royalist and High Church. Clarendon, who was the dominant minister of the Crown, was the avowed apostle of no toleration, and lost no time in using his power to put his theories into operation. The Act of Uniformity, with the other measures of the famous Clarendon Code, were to have tremendous, if unforeseen, consequences in both the ecclesiastical and political spheres. Not the least of these was the forcing of an alliance between the ejected Presbyterian clergy and the despised separatists, an alliance which, in fact, marked the birth of Nonconformity as a definite and vital factor in the national life. Thenceforward the established Church of England was stranded high and dry in a peculiar position of isolation, cut off alike from Rome, from the Protestants of Europe, and from a very large number of religious people within the borders of the realm. It was unfortunate that this isolation should have arisen out of the close association between the Church and the Court, for in the intense reaction of the time, from the former régime of strict Puritanism, the Church itself became tainted with the Court's laxity. By its emergence as a political force and its renewed adoption of the rôle of persecutor, it tended to over-emphasize its secular function at the expense of its spiritual one. The dissenting minority on the other hand nurtured its grievances in an atmosphere of censoriousness and pharisaism, and, being excluded by law from taking part in official and public life, it developed a narrow morality equally subversive of spiritual force. Both were the poorer for this rigorous policy of separation.

For more than a decade after the passing of the Act of Uniformity, the Anglican Church was in a position to enjoy its triumph undisturbed. It was not until the nation awoke to the dangerous possibilities indicated by the Duke of York's attraction to the Roman Church and again raised the cry of "No Popery," that the apologists of the establishment had once more to adopt a defensive attitude. The revival of strong anti-Papal feeling in the public mind, which was reflected in the Test Acts, was accentuated by the Duke's open avowal of Roman Catholicism. It culminated in the panic aroused by the amazing fabrications of the Popish plot, and was the signal for a parallel revival of

Anglican apologetic writings. Learned doctors on all hands strove to point the moral and adorn the tale by setting forth the excellencies of the establishment, and vilifying those who dared to suggest any possible curtailment of monarchical power either by popular government or Papal supremacy.

Dr. John Nalson's volume on *The Common Interest of King and People*, published in 1677, was an expression of contemporary Anglican thought, inasmuch as in it the author declared emphatically against the heresy " of those persons who make laws to have a priority before kings and governors; as if the laws made kings and magistrates, when in truth God and Nature vested primogeniture with the right of kings and magistrates, and they made the first laws. This is a mistake of such dangerous consequence," he added, " that if it comes to be allowed and popular it robs all kings of the most valuable jewel in their crowns which was set there by God himself, who set them upon their heads, *viz.*, a Divine Right and Title to their sovereignty and dominion." Nalson's views on Papal supremacy were equally strong, for he declared that it would divest the Prince of sovereignty no less than the people of liberty. His argument was based on the utilitarian doctrine that the end of all government is the happiness of society, and its function lies in the protection of the lives and property of its subjects and the exercise of distributive justice. Any merit which might be found in his discussion of law and the theory of representative assemblies is subject to a discount in the light of the nauseating

THE BACKGROUND

superlatives which he employed in the latter half of his book, to extol the glories of the English Constitution and the moral perfection of the English king. He was on his own confession (in a letter to Sancroft, 14th July, 1683), a place-hunter, and the acknowledgment of sycophantic motives inevitably detracts from the value of his political speculations.

Talk of the exclusion of the Duke of York from the throne, as the only means of defence for English Protestantism, had been in the air since the end of 1673; but not until the villainous Oates stirred up popular feeling into a frenzy did the idea crystallize in the Exclusion Bill. The problem of the succession then became the dominating political issue for the next three years. The High Church party, as ever, threw all its weight into the support of the royal cause, and spared no effort to ensure that the lawful hereditary succession should remain unbroken. But at the same time its members expressed in the strongest terms their abhorrence of any kind of foreign interference, whether Papal or otherwise, in English affairs. They were faced with the embarrassing necessity of defending a thesis at a time when its working out in practical politics threatened not only to involve the nation in disaster, but simultaneously to bring about the eclipse of the party itself.

In 1679, while the controversy was at its fiercest, a number of political writings by Sir Robert Filmer were reprinted in a posthumous collection. The most important of these were *The Freeholders' Grand Inquest*, which was intended as a manual of citizenship or guide to electors; and *The Anarchy of a Limited or Mixed Monarchy*, in which he declared that "Monarchy hath been crucified (as it were) between two thieves, the Pope and the People," and "the main and indeed the only point of Popery is the alienating and withdrawing of subjects from their obedience to their Prince, to raise sedition and rebellion." His most famous work, *Patriarcha*, did not appear in print until the following year. Although the theory of absolute sovereignty and the subordination of Parliament to the king, which was the theme of all his writings, was due to the inspiration of the first Charles, the dates of these publications and the measure of their popularity are significant of the course of events in the time of the second.

Among the writings actually inspired by the excitement of the time, perhaps Falkner's *Christian Loyalty* stated the High Church position as powerfully and lucidly as any. In the first part of his book, Falkner was at pains to define Royal supremacy, especially in relation to ecclesiastical affairs. That his point of view had suffered modification by the events of which his generation had been such anxious witnesses, is shown by his endeavour to reconcile his views on monarchical supremacy with the claims made to private rights by citizens and to ecclesiastical privilege by the Church. To effect this reconciliation, he pointed out that the possession of supreme governorship did not necessarily involve the right or duty of performing all the offices of a subordinate, nor could it legalize the interference with

THE BACKGROUND

property rights of individuals or of the Church. That the sovereign power, while supreme in temporal affairs, must be exercised within the limits of the laws of Nature is axiomatic. The prince is none the less supreme when the consent of his subjects is taken before the enactment of new laws in Parliament. "Man hath not a less but a greater government over himself when he guideth himself by the Rules of Reason, nor is it therefore any diminution of the power of a governor when the exercise thereof is and ought to be managed by rules of common equity."[1] The phrase, "ought to be," employed in that sentence symbolizes the change in attitude which English thought had unconsciously experienced during the middle years of the seventeenth century.

While Falkner definitely rejected the Presbyterian contention that the direct authority of Christ given to ministers of religion places them outside the sphere of subjection to civil magistrates or kings, he asserted that the ecclesiastical jurisdiction of the monarch could only be exercised within certain limits. Sovereign power cannot alter matters of faith, order and worship in the Church. "The spiritual authority of the ecclesiastical officers is of a distinct nature from the secular power, and is no way prejudicial to royal supremacy,"[2] and "as it is not derived from any temporal power, neither may it be taken away or abolished thereby."[3] This point

---
[1] *Christian Loyalty*, William Falkner, preacher at St. Nicholas, Lyme Regis, 1679, p. 11.
[2] *Christian Loyalty*, p. 27.   [3] *Ibid*, p. 17.

was of the utmost importance in the stand taken by the Nonjuring bishops against the deprivation order made by William in 1689-90; and its underlying conception of the Church as a spiritual society with a life of its own apart from that of the secular state, was the basis upon which they founded their claim to continued existence as the true original Anglican Church.

The passage in *Christian Loyalty* concerning indefeasible hereditary right might well have come from the pen of a Nonjuror ten years later, so exactly does it state the position of the anti-revolutionists. " No just right of supremacy or any part of royalty can be gained by possession upon an unjust title against the right owner upon a sure title; this being a parallel case to a thief being possessed of an honest man's goods. No sovereign king (unless by voluntarily relinquishing his whole authority to the next heir) can transfer his royal supremacy to any other person whomsoever, partly because the divine constitution, having placed supremacy in the chief secular governors, God expecteth from them a due care of managing of this power for the good of his people . . . partly also because the constitutions of the Realm oblige all subjects thereof to maintain the royalties of the Crown and to perform faith and true allegiance not only to the king in being, but also to his heirs and successors . . . and partly because we are a free-born people and not slaves, that mastery can pass from one to another over us according to any one person's pleasure."[1] From this also follows

[1] *Christian Loyalty*, pp. 233-4.

Falkner's dictum that "the asserting of supremacy of government in the body of the people is a position big with nonsense and irreligion,"[1] but, although he stoutly denied any Papal claims to supremacy, he believed that if a General Council of the Western Churches were ever in being it would not constitute a foreign jurisdiction (being partly English in constitution) and would, therefore, have a claim on the allegiance of English Churchmen, so long as it did not "abridge or violate the royal authority."

The subject of toleration and liberty of conscience was treated in *Christian Loyalty* in a manner which the author's opponents would doubtless call bigoted, and his friends deem finely ironical. He could find no *via media* between Anglicanism and anarchy if all men were to be allowed to choose between a State religion and one formulated by the inner light of their own conscience. His adherence to the authoritarian point of view led him to the remarkable conclusion that, as even a heathen rule has been known to have given active support to true religion, how much more, therefore (by inference) would a Catholic monarch, if such should ever reign, endeavour to support the Anglican Church as the institution which best helped to achieve the true end of government. Falkner was more precise than some of his contemporaries in formulating what the true end of government should be, namely, the good of the people, and his emphasis on morality as a political end, and religion as a means to its achieve-

[1] *Christian Loyalty*, p. 292.

ment, marks him as being the forerunner of a later rather than the survivor of an earlier phase of speculation. " It being generally acknowledged," he wrote, " that the secular authority is to take care that justice, honesty, peace and virtue be established and preserved in the world, even from hence we may infer the necessity of its care about matters of religion."[1]

In the second part of his book, Falkner declared that excommunication did not *ipso facto* involve forfeiture of civil rights, although temporal disabilities might be added by the civil magistrates to an ecclesiastical sentence; but in no case could any man be relieved of the obligation of obedience and duty to his sovereign. This view he modified slightly when he made the hesitating admission that, while the defence of religion could not justify resistance to the sovereign, the well-nigh unthinkable case of conspiracy by the ruler to ruin the State might relieve the subjects of their due obedience if they could thus be enabled to preserve the State itself intact.

Apart from this somewhat doubtful exception, Falkner's discussion of passive obedience and non-resistance was carried on in the familiar terms employed by all the Anglican divines of his day, whose abhorrence of the very thought of resistance was the natural corollary to their passionate belief in Divine Right. When, in 1689, the Nonjurors came to state their faith and defend their position, they had not to create a case so much as to sustain a

[1] *Christian Loyalty*, p. 116.

tradition. Their virtue, if virtue it was, took the form of unswerving fidelity to the principles of Church and State which they inherited from the accumulated store of Anglo-Catholic[1] philosophy.

[1] In the *Political History of England*, Vol. VII, p. 128-9, the phrase " Anglo-Catholic " is used to designate the High Church party in the time of the first Stuart King.

CHAPTER II

THE NONJURING CHURCH

1. *James II. and the Anglican Church.*

THE debt which James II. owed to those staunch members of the Anglican Church who, by throwing all their weight against the Exclusion Bills, had helped to set him on the English throne, soon dwindled into insignificance beside the debt which he owed to them for keeping him there. That he succeeded his brother as simply and unostentatiously as he did was due largely to the unexpectedness of Charles' death, and to his own promptitude in declaring publicly within an hour of the event that he would make it his endeavour "to preserve this government both in Church and State as it is now by law established." But this promise, repeated at the opening of Parliament three months later, did not prevent him from encouraging the Jesuits in their multifarious activities ; from openly associating with them and other Roman Catholics as much in their worship as in the everyday life at Court ; or from embarking upon a series of actions everyone of which was calculated to rouse the greatest antagonism among the clergy of the Establishment and most of which were, whether by accident or design, subversive of the Constitution. The cumulative effects of those proceedings would have worn down the patience of the Church in a much shorter time than three years, had the clergy not been nurtured in the rigorous mental environment of passive obedience.

Archbishop Sancroft, with Ken and other eminent ecclesiastics had attended Charles at his death-bed, and in spite of his refusal of their ministrations and of the new King's avowed Catholicism, they were still convinced that the maintenance of the English Church and the doctrine of indefeasible hereditary right were mutually dependent conceptions. Hence for three stormy years the Church endured the persecutions of the King who, having been brought up in the traditions of his grandfather to believe in his own divine right and to expect nothing but loyalty from the Establishment, was unable to anticipate the effect occasioned in the mind of his people by his deliberate attempt to live up to the one after having alienated the other. Had James been able to understand that popular belief in the Divine Right of Kings was a fruit produced by and nourished in the national Church, and that any attack on the parent growth would inevitably weaken and ultimately destroy the product, he might have proceeded with his interference in ecclesiastical affairs with at least a show of legality and caution. But he was blind to that simple fact, and could not realize that every gesture indicative of his own Romanism and his contempt for the Anglican Communion was followed by a reaction tending to weaken, if not altogether to break down, the old unquestioning support of the Crown.

In order to deal with the case of Bishop Compton, who had merited his displeasure, but had committed no offence either ecclesiastical or civil, the King re-established the Court of High Commission. The suspension of the Bishop, by this Court, from the exercise of his episcopal functions followed close on his exclusion from the Privy Council, and this latter punishment was also meted out to the Archbishop for his refusal to serve as a member of the illegal court.

The King not only consistently refused to appoint nominees of the Archbishop and his colleagues to the sees and other ecclesiastical offices under the royal gift which fell vacant, but insisted on the induction of his own candidate to many of the most important posts. A Roman Catholic was instituted to the deanery of Christ Church, Oxford, and other university appointments were granted to men excused by special warrant from the necessity of taking the sacrament or subscribing to the oaths. His dealings with the Master and Fellows of Magdalen College from March 1687 over a period of nine months until the foundation was turned into a Catholic Seminary under the headship of the Roman Bishop Madura, were but the culminating acts of his aggressive policy against the University.[1]

The popularity of Monmouth and the horror aroused by Jeffreys' Bloody Assize had at the outset of the reign combined to weaken in the minds of the

[1] See Macaulay, *History of England*, Vol. II, pp. 97–115 (Edinburgh edition).

THE NONJURING CHURCH

rank and file of Anglican Churchmen their insistence upon passive obedience; while Louis XIV.'s treatment of the Huguenots, culminating in his revocation of the Edict of Nantes in October, 1685, had given to the mass of the population in England a vision of the kind of fate which might be theirs at the hands of a Roman Catholic autocrat. The rising tide of resentment and anxiety felt by all parties was deepened by the King's direct violation of the Test Act in granting commissions in the Army to avowed Romanists. The use of the dispensing power in any sphere was dangerous. Anybody with more insight into the probable effects of his actions than James possessed would have known that its use in any religious connection would, in the light of current public opinion, be fatal. The faculty which the King possessed of alienating those who by tradition and desire were his natural and loyal supporters was of that quality which, had it been employed in the worthier arts of statesmanship, would have stamped him at once as a genius.

Not content with his direct attack on the Church, James sought, behind her back, to buy the support of her enemies. The Declarations of Indulgence which he issued in April 1687 and in the succeeding year, far outreached that of Charles II. in their unconstitutional character. The second of these declarations was the final straw which broke the patience of the Establishment. In seeking to buy a recognized place in public life for his friends of the Roman communion at the price of the grant of similar privileges for the Presbyterians and other dissenters, he lost what had been and might still have proved to be for him the priceless possession of the loyalty of the great majority of his subjects. The trial of the Seven Bishops was the immediate cause of the sending of the invitation to William of Orange; the letter requesting his presence in England was, significantly enough, signed on the same day upon which the Bishops were acquitted.[1] The rejoicing of the population of London on hearing of the result of the trial was a forecast of the triumph of the Revolution. That five of the seven were afterwards among the leaders of that remnant of the Anglican Church which refused to acknowledge the Revolution Settlement, was not an inconsistency of principle which a cursory thought might indicate. Sancroft, Ken, Turner, Lake, and White, in carrying their protest to the point at which they preferred to incur the King's wrath and to endure imprisonment in the Tower rather than read his declaration, were thereby vindicating their unshakable belief in the validity of the individual conscience, and the spiritual autonomy of the Anglican Church, no less than in the inviolable character of the English Constitution. Bound up in the very texture of conscience was the sacredness of their oaths. Bound up in the essential nature of the Constitution was the doctrine of indefeasible hereditary right. The Bishops' acceptance of imprisonment in June, 1688, and of deprivation a year and a half later were acts shaped to the same pattern. It is possible to argue that they were mistaken in one or the other or in both cases,

[1] June 30th, 1688.

but the charge of inconsistency is not one which can bear close examination.

But for two months after the trial of the Bishops the King pursued his course and deluded himself into the belief that he was still safe. It was not until September that he began to realize the width of the breach which he had made with the Anglican Church. The frantic endeavours which he then made to win back her confidence by granting concession after concession and withdrawing several of the more obnoxious of his orders and institutions were too late to avail. Coming at such a time, the exclusion of the Roman Catholics from the House of Commons, the restoration of Bishop Compton to his see, and the Fellows of Magdalen to their college, and the abolition of the Court of High Commission were not sufficient guarantee of the King's good faith. The Bishops, headed by Sancroft, were, either separately or in conjunction with the secular peers, in direct communication with James at least five times between the early days of September and the end of November, offering their advice and beseeching him to renounce the dispensing power and call an immediate Parliament. He rejected their requests with as little regard as he listened to their counsel until the last time of all, when, already contemplating his own flight, he reluctantly consented to issue writs for the election. It is reported that even when in Salisbury, when the catastrophe of the Revolution against his throne was already half accomplished, the King was rash enough to demand the use of the Bishop's private chapel for the celebration of Mass, and the Anglican building would have been the scene of the Roman service, had not the Bishop's chaplain defiantly denied the right of the Roman priest to administer the sacrament there.

To the end, therefore, the King made no gesture of conciliation that could have earned the respect of the clergy for the official secular head of their national Church. Nonconformists of all shades, from Papists to Quakers, had received more favours at his hands than had the members of the one Church which had legal right to his consideration. It was small wonder that the great majority of the clergy welcomed the advent in England of one who, even if his Protestantism was of too Latitudinarian a variety to earn wholehearted approval, gave in his integrity of character some sort of pledge that his avowed intent of fostering the National Church would be no empty promise, but would lead to the rehabilitation of that Church in her former position of prestige and influence.

2. *The " State Point."*

Bishop Compton, who had suffered so much at the instigation of James II., was the only ecclesiastic who signed the invitation which was sent to William of Orange in the summer of 1688. The Archbishop, with various members of the episcopal bench had on more than one occasion in the latter half of that year expressly denied to the King the complicity of the clergy in the acts of the Revolutionary party. But after the duress of James' ill-timed persecution,

THE NONJURING CHURCH

there was little trace left of the servility which had marked the relationship between the spiritual peers and the earlier Stuart Kings.

When the Convention called by William met in London on January 22nd, the allegiance of the bishops to the theory of indefeasible hereditary right was still to all intents and purposes unbroken, but they realized that the Church whose servants they were could, even if allowed a legal existence, barely fulfil her function in the life of the nation under a Roman Catholic monarch who deliberately aimed at her discomfiture. They had to decide upon their line of action in face of the apparently irreconcilable necessities of Church and State. While the decision was still unmade, Jeremy Collier, afterwards a bishop in the Nonjuring Church, came under the penalty of the law for a pamphlet in which he stated " We have an excellent Church, and we do well to take due care to continue its Establishment, but to dispossess our Prince upon this score has as little divinity as law in it. To endeavour to preserve our religion by such methods will make it more fatal to us in the event than Atheism itself. 'Tis a mistake to think the world was meant for none but Protestants, and if Dominion was founded in grace, I'm afraid our share would not be great in the division."[1] To those who imagined that the Revolution would save the Church as well as the State the expression of such views must have been little short of exasperating. To those who accepted

[1] *The Desertion Discussed in a Letter to a Country Gentleman*, 1688.

the statement, with all its political and ecclesiastical implications, the Revolution was not only a grave blunder, but also a damnable sin. There were bishops and clergy in both camps.

The overwhelming majority of the clergy were still unable to consider, much less to accept, any plan of government whereby James would be excluded from the throne. Some were anxious for his return—a return to be safeguarded by guarantees for the protection of the Church and Constitution. Others approved of the plan for a Regency, whereby the King was to be declared unfit to reign and the administration was to be given by Parliament into the hands of a Regent, but the King was not to be (because as King he could not be) deprived of his title. A few supported Danby's plan, by which James wa sto be regarded as having abdicated, and Mary, as his next heir, was to be crowned Queen forthwith. These plans were doomed to failure for the plain reasons, that, with reference to the first, no guarantees which James might offer would be worth anything more than the paper on which they were written; in the second place, William, who, as the rescuer of the country from a tyrant and as a very able administrator, was the obvious candidate for the regency, would have nothing to do with the idea; and thirdly, Mary definitely refused to counter any suggestion which should bring about her own exaltation above the position of her husband.

When the Convention first met, the plea of abdication was not one which could earn the general approval of the Church. " To abdicate an office

THE NONJURING CHURCH 43

always supposes the consent of him who quits it."[1] wrote Collier, but in the case in point the loyal Churchmen were not ready to be convinced of James' consent, and were only too anxious to condone him. " There were such terrible disorders in the kingdom, and all places were either flaming or ready to take fire. What should a Prince do, when he had scarce anything left him to lose but himself, but consult his safety and give way to the inevitable evil ? "[2] In this view, James had been forced to fly for his life or, in other words, William as an usurper had driven the King out of his kingdom. Thus far it was possible for both sections of the Church to find agreement without putting their principles to too great a strain, for James was still the rightful possessor of the crown. Where Anglicans differed was on the question whether obedience was due to the *de jure* or to the *de facto* King. Strict adherence to the doctrine of Sovereignty as a divine gift and its corollary of passive obedience led the High Churchmen to reject the possibility of its transfer by force of arms or other revolutionary methods. To him in whom the rightful authority resided was their obedience due for ever. When the Convention, after much debating, declared that King James had abdicated, that the throne was vacant, and that William should therefore assume the title to the authority which he was already in fact exercising, the rest of the clergy bowed before the storm and decided for the *de facto* King. The decision of the

[1] *The Desertion Discussed in a Letter to a Country Gentleman.*
[2] *Ibid.*

Convention was, as Leslie pointed out years afterwards, in some senses a triumph for the Church over the Whigs, who by striving to base the Revolution on the power of the people to reject as well as to choose their own sovereign would have reduced it to the level of 1648, and thus alienated an even greater number of the Tories and Churchmen than in fact they did. "You see here the reason why the Convention went upon the point of abdication," he wrote, "it was on purpose to avoid that of coercion which they knew to be contrary to all known laws of the land. Therefore they voted that the King had renounced his crown, and that with the manifest intention of his own mind and will . . . and that this renouncing was what they meant by abdication."[1] Those who afterwards refused the oaths imposed by the Convention based their refusal on the principle that, whereas James had a perfect right to fly for his own safety, his acting upon that right could in no sense absolve his subjects from their obedience to him. His right to their allegiance was inseparable from his right to govern; both were from God and neither could be abdicated because they were ordained by God for the benefit of all concerned.

Archbishop Sancroft made his last public appearance at the Council of Peers called by William in London on the 21st December, on which occasion he seemed to favour the idea of recalling the fleeing King. Between the two sessions of this Council, news of the King's escape to France reached London. At the second session the Primate was not present.

[1] *The Rehearsal*, IV, 8; October 30th, 1708.

THE NONJURING CHURCH

He therefore took no part in the address to William, asking him to administer the Government and to call a free Parliament. By the time the Convention met a month later, the Archbishop, still champion of the Jacobite cause, was the sponsor of the Regency scheme. Had he attended the debates of the Convention, it is possible that his moderating influence might have enabled the House of Lords to withstand the revolutionary resolutions of the Commons and to have stood firm for the retention by James of his royal title, even if not for his recall. Almost all the bishops and many other peers who were present at the sittings of the Convention were still anxious not to break the direct line of succession, and, though admittedly open to criticism in other directions, the idea of a Regency at least in theory prevented such a break. But the authority which had called the Convention was one which the Archbishop could not acknowledge, and he declined to attend. His position was indeed one of almost unimaginable difficulty, as his biographer afterwards recognized. "Attachment to the Protestant cause was known to be a master principle of his mind. No one could have been more convinced than he was of the fixed and gloomy bigotry of James, of the general insincerity of his character, of his fixed design to establish Popery in the kingdom, and of the impossibility of relying on his promises and assertions. Thus he must have felt as strongly as anyone could do the evils connected with retaining that monarch on the throne; but still from feeling that his right to that throne was indefeasible he would not consent to his exclusion."[1] The mystery which surrounds his curious abstention from the public leadership of the Church in that day of her great need, an abstention so unexpected after the boldness of his attitude towards the King's illegal acts, and so foreign to the nature of one who had never been, and still refused to be, afraid of evil consequences accruing to himself as leader, can be accounted for only by one of two possibilities. The Archbishop may have been by his age or some other physical disability, at that time incapable of making great decisions or assuming grave responsibility; his early retirement into private life after the Revolution was accomplished gives colour to this view, though the short time which had elapsed since he had had the temerity to tender good advice to James detracts from it. More probably he had become aware at a late hour of the deficiencies of his own scheme for a Regency, and while he was far too honest a man to defend anything which he once saw to be wrong, he was yet not strong enough to cause the withdrawal of the plan once it had been officially adopted by other influential Tory peers.

The refusal of the Archbishop and eight other bishops to take the oaths prescribed to members of both Houses by the Act which converted the Convention into a Parliament, was a definite indication that the events of the Revolution were to prove a stumbling block to the cause of unity in the National Church. His resignation from the Privy Council and withdrawal from the public

[1] D'Oyley's *Life of Sancroft*, Vol. II, p. 81.

THE NONJURING CHURCH

exercise of his archiepiscopal functions in connection with the consecration of Gilbert Burnet to the see of Salisbury, and the Coronation of the King and Queen were further signs of the cleavage. But it was not until the Parliament enacted that the new oaths of Allegiance and Supremacy were to be made obligatory on all who held ecclesiastical or academical preferment, that the extent of the divergence in Anglican opinion and practice became fully realized. Over four hundred persons refused the oaths and placed themselves under the ban of suspension on August 1st, 1689. Very few of these recanted their refusal during the six months' grace allowed by Parliament; the great majority therefore were deprived of office by its authority on February 1st following.

3. *The " Church Point."*

The refusal of the oaths was the "State Point" which brought to a definite issue the cleavage between the High Church Tories on the one hand, and the combination of their less exacting brethren of the Low Church with the triumphant Whigs on the other. But the controversy which this division engendered might have survived only as a very minor political sensation, had it not also involved the " Church Point," or deprivations.

These deprivations were carried out without the semblance of ecclesiastical authority, and, emanating from the purely secular court of Parliament as they did, they were in the eyes of the High Church Party absolutely illegal and void. When, in course of time, the sees of the deprived bishops were filled (again by the secular authority) the new holders, by accepting office not legally vacant, came to be regarded as anti-bishops and therefore as the creators of a schism in the Church. The contention made by Sancroft and his colleagues that, as their authority was from Christ and could, therefore, only be removed by him or his appointed deputies on grounds of heresy or gross misconduct, and could never in any case be surrendered to a lay power, was correct according to the doctrine of their Church. The authority received by them at their consecration was granted in order that they might exercise it for the spiritual welfare of their flocks. This authority had not been rescinded by its original giver, and they were, therefore, under an obligation of the most sacred kind to continue their expression of it by continuing the ministrations of his Church. Holding this conviction, they could not in honesty, quite apart from other considerations, attach themselves in a lay capacity to that portion of the Church which had declined from their views and had accepted the Revolution settlement in ecclesiastical as well as political affairs. Another factor in the situation was the use in the Revolution Church of the so-called "immoral prayers," in the phraseology of which William and Mary were acknowledged as King and Queen. The loyal High Churchmen, however much they might desire to see their Church saved from the persecutions of a Romish King, could never cease to pray for James and his direct heirs and

THE NONJURING CHURCH 49

successors as the rightful King of England. They had no option but to continue worshipping in their own way, and to perpetuate by the consecration of new bishops the Church of which they were the Fathers in God.

It was inevitable that the association of the name of King James with the origin and liturgy of the Nonjuring Church should expose the members thereof to the charge of being Jacobites. In fact, their attitude towards the Jacobite cause disclosed a wide difference of opinion. Bishop Cartwright, of Chester, though technically a Nonjuror in that he refused the oaths, had been politically so far attached to the cause of James that he went into exile with his royal master; but there was so much of the plotter and so little of the priest in his composition that he was never a member of the Nonjuring Church. Turner, of Ely, was probably the most ardent Jacobite among those five who, after the deaths of Thomas and Lake, formed with the Archbishop the original hierarchy of the Nonjuring communion. He was found to be implicated in a restoration plot, and was exiled. At the other extreme were Frampton and Ken. The former continued his attendance at the Parish Church after his deprivation, and even continued to hold a small living, though ousted from his bishopric. Ken, though he refused the oaths, did so with great reluctance and spared no effort to heal the schism in the Church. When, in 1710, he and Lloyd were the sole survivors of the original Nonjuring episcopate, he made a final, though a vain attempt to effect a reconciliation between the two sections of the Anglican Church by acknowledging his successor at Bath and Wells, and abandoning his own use of his ecclesiastical title.

This action was the cause of much distress to his more ardent brethren. Hickes wrote of Ken's " strange humour of resigning . . strange humour first, because it was not in his power so much as to make a cession without the consent of his colleagues, much less without their consent to resign to any particular person, because by the nature of the Episcopal College as well as the canons of the Church they were to elect and admit into his vacant see. Secondly, because he pretended to resign in order to heal the schism in his diocese ; a reason which, if good, should have obliged him to resign at first and not to have kept his diocese twelve years or more in schism. Thirdly . . . because he resigns to one with whom he does not communicate upon the account of the immoral prayers ; whereby the Bishop to whom he resigned effectually teaches the flock which he resigned to him the damnable doctrine of resistance and deposing sovereign princes."[1] It is as impossible to escape Hickes' relentless argument as it is to resent the saintly Bishop's genuine desire to heal the breach in the Church. But what may have seemed a tendency to weakness on Ken's part was probably condoned by his fellow Nonjurors in view both of the transparent purity of his character and of his strenuous efforts to help those among his

[1] A letter to Mr. Nelson, reprinted in *The Constitution of the Catholic Church*.

THE NONJURING CHURCH 51

brethren who were plunged into economic distress through their deprivation.

That such distress should befall many of those who lost the emoluments of their ecclesiastical or academical office was inevitable. Samuel Grascome drew a vivid picture of their sufferings. "There has been severity enough used to the Nonjurors; their estates have been taken from them, their persons exposed to the mob. They are made the contempt and scorn of mankind, they suffer injuries without redress . . . yet they say they are willing to live quietly if they may be suffered so to do. But if the Government think they have not suffered enough already they must be content to suffer more; they have no other remedy but to appeal and apply themselves to God."[1] Leslie seems to have taken a certain amount of pride in an opponent's reference to the "tattered gowns and slouching hats" of those who were against the policy of "resistance which provides plentifully for its followers."[2] The poverty of the Nonjurors was at least a token of the sincerity of their convictions on the political issue; but poverty added to uncertainty may have led some to adopt a way of living which could not but diminish the respect in which they were held by members of their own Church and was sure to earn for them the taunts of those "jolly swearers,"[3] whose convenient consciences had not obliged them to renounce their livelihoods at the call of consistency

---
[1] *Moderation in Fashion.*
[2] *The Good Old Cause Further Discussed.*
[3] Grascome's appellation of those who took the oaths, in his *Brief Answer to a Late Discourse.*

52 ALLEGIANCE IN CHURCH AND STATE

of conviction. A party is not to be judged by the actions, good or bad, of a small minority among its membership. The holiness of Ken or Kettlewell and the vehemence of Hickes or Leslie were certainly contributory factors of great importance to the life of the Nonjuring Church, but in themselves they were not qualities common to every member of it any more than the reported immorality or hypocrisy of individuals which formed the subject of references by Dr. Johnson or Colley Cibber were typical of the whole body.

The existence of the Nonjuring Church as a separate communion was based originally upon the honest strength of its members' convictions regarding the wrongness of the oaths and the invalidity of lay control in ecclesiastical affairs. The "State Point" inevitably lost its driving power in course of time when it became obvious that the Declaration of Right and the Act of Settlement were no ephemeral outcome of party politics, but were firmly woven into the very stuff of the Constitution. The direct Stuart line would not renounce Roman Catholicism and therefore could never return to the throne of England, for, whatever else the Parliament disputed, there was never any doubt about its wholehearted rejection of a Popish head for the State and Church of England. Hence, although the Government twice (after the death of James II. in 1700, and again in 1715) saw fit to impose an oath of Abjuration calling upon holders of office who were required to take the usual oath of Allegiance explicitly to renounce the claims of James' descendants, the ranks of Nonjurors were

THE NONJURING CHURCH 53

only increased by eleven through the advent of Nonabjurors. Even with the addition of a few "Penitents" who recanted their oaths upon more mature consideration, the recorded additions from outside to the membership of the Nonjuring Church failed by a considerable margin to balance the numbers of those who left it to comply with the Government.[1] After the accession of the House of Hanover the perpetuation of a separate communion on political grounds became a bad habit rather than a matter of conviction. No reasonable defence can be found for it.

Neither could the "Church Point" be pleaded as a valid reason for perpetuating the division. The Nonjurors' claim that the Revolution Church was the schismatical body, implied that, conversely, they were themselves the Established Church. But though it was difficult, if not impossible, as Stillingfleet acknowledged[2] to find a logical weakness in their defence of this claim as it was at first put forward, it was patently absurd to regard as the National Church an impotent and dwindling company which owned as its earthly head a man who was not only of alien communion but was also an exile from, and the political enemy of, the State in which that Church claimed to be established. The insistence on the separate organization of the Nonjuring Church in 1689 was the strong action of men bent on

---

[1] Overton, in *The Nonjurors, Their Lives, Principles and Writings*, gives the numbers as following: Nonabjurors 11, Penitents 16, Compliers 41.

[2] In his *Vindication of His Majesty's Authority to Fill the Vacant Sees*, 1691.

vindicating their faith in the Church's right to spiritual autonomy; it was a reasonable protest against the unjustifiable substitution of lay for ecclesiastical control in religious affairs. The perpetuation of that organization beyond the lifetime of the last of the deprived bishops, or, at latest, the lifetime of those consecrated before the accession of Queen Anne, was the act of childishness committed by those who took themselves so seriously that they would not recognize accomplished facts as facts, if such failed to fit into their preconceived notions. Nevertheless, twenty-seven in all were consecrated bishops of the Nonjuring Church between the years 1694 and 1795, including two whose work lay in America, and seven who were bishops of the seceders after the Usages controversy. A number of Nonjuring congregations had regular meeting places in London.[1] There were similar oratories scattered about in the provinces where a wealthy lay Nonjuror allowed the use of his private chapel or where there was a sufficient number of members to give the necessary support.

The Revolution of 1689, although it brought into prominence the political opinions of the High Church Party and was the proximate cause of the separation between that Party and the avowedly Protestant Church of England, cannot in any sense be said to have been the original cause of those opinions. The controversies which it aroused grew out of the latent

---

[1] Overton mentions thirteen by name, apart from private houses, but refers to a letter sent to Archbishop Wake in 1716, giving the number as fifty.

THE NONJURING CHURCH 55

divergencies of view between the two sections of the Church. The Nonjurors were the direct political offspring of James I. Their kinship was with Laud, Filmer, Faulkner, and all other Anglo-Catholics who throughout the seventeenth century had preached and practised non-resistance, extolled the Divine Right of Kings, asserted the arbitrary nature of sovereignty, and founded their speculations on the scriptural account of the divine origin of government in the patriarchal organization of society, without absorbing a taint of the popular or Puritan views on the contract and the authority of the people. At no point did they deviate from the direction which Anglican orthodoxy had adopted as its own. They developed the doctrines which they found to hand in a manner determined by the circumstances of their day, but the faith was not of their making, it was their inheritance. That which they received they did not suffer to be diminished either by arguments of expediency or any personal suffering and loss.

CHAPTER III

THE ORIGIN AND AIMS OF MONARCHICAL GOVERNMENT

1. *Monarchy.*

AMID all the political controversy engendered by the Revolution of 1688, there was never any serious doubt cast by either section of the Anglican Church on the pre-eminence of monarchy as an instrument of government. Monarchy as the core of the English Constitution was taken for granted. Interminable arguments concerning the method of succession, the nature of authority and its original source, raged between the two parties, but there was fundamental agreement about the basic rightness of Kingship. Monarchy was the express institution of God, and all other forms of government were contrary to his known will. In a phrase of Hickes " Kings are God's Vicegerents upon earth, and the supreme, especially the Royal, power is the ordinance of God."[1] Commonwealths and democratic governments had their births among pagan peoples, and were not only dangerous but sinful, and the Anglican politician was not slow to draw illustrations of their wickedness from the experiences through which his Church and

[1] Sermon preached at Bow Church, before the Lord Mayor of London, 1682.

country had passed in the middle years of the century. Aristocracies led to faction and strife no less certainly than did popular government. It was acknowledged that the bad government of Princes or the licentiousness of peoples had on occasion merited punishment by the overthrow of established order in favour of one of these debased forms, but in the experience of England such incidents were in the nature of a political disease and were not regarded as valid arguments against the institution of monarchy itself, an institution which was so much an integral part of Anglican political theory that it was accepted without discussion.

2. *The Succession.*

The historical events which gave rise to the Non-juring Party in English politics suggest that the subject of indefeasible hereditary right was one which would naturally occupy a prominent place in the writings of the group. There had indeed already been strong pronouncements made by various members of it at the time of the controversy over the Exclusion Bills. In the introduction to his *Jovian* (1683), Hickes wrote "If the Imperial crown of England be subject to none but God, then, to endeavour to exclude the whole royal line to prevent Popery, would be opposition to the will of God. So to exclude any one person of the Royal family, but most of all the next heir upon the line, from the absolute right or birthright which God alone hath given him, would be also to oppose the will of God."

The return of the Stuarts after the series of governmental experiments carried on in England between 1648-1660 had been to the mind of the Anglican Church an obvious and triumphant vindication of this doctrine of primogeniture. In the restoration of " his chosen servant Charles " to the throne of his fathers after twelve years of exile, God had given to his faithful Church yet one more proof of his eternal principle of government, a principle traceable by any careful student who chose to examine the providential relationship of God to man from the days of Adam to the year of grace, 1689.

But whereas the desperate situation caused by James II.'s mis-handling of Church and State affairs, and accentuated by his flight, was sufficient inducement to the Low Church Party to abandon their strict adhesion to the theory of primogeniture, in order to avail themselves of the services of the Prince of Orange to restore order and liberty to the Country ; the bare fact of the break in the regular succession caused by William's accession to the throne was in itself sufficient condemnation of the Revolution in the eyes of the Anglo-Catholics. Primogeniture was, in their view, the direct ordinance of the God whom they served. If the Popish practices of James threatened to bring ruin on the Church and realm of England, then doubtless such a catastrophe, if unavoidable by legitimate means, must be interpreted as part of the inscrutable mystery of God who chose to punish sinful men through the misdeeds of his servant the King. But the result of misrule, however disastrous, could not in itself justify the denial by any man of his loyalty to God's law. Common sense might demand that William should save the Protestant cause in England, and that the monarchy should be limited and constitutional instead of despotic and absolute, but conscience demanded even more insistently that God should be trusted and oaths in his name should be preserved inviolate.

While the Nonjurors pointed to the divine origin of primogeniture related in the Old Testament narrative, they acknowledged that its practice in England was only to be traced to the Middle Ages. It was a legacy from the Germanic peoples transmitted to English law by the Norman Conquest, and developed through the feudal system. They met the challenge of their opponents, that in point of fact the English crown had *not* descended in unbroken succession, but had changed from family to family, by the explanation that, while it was God's plan that monarchical government should descend from father to son in direct line, the detailed working of such a scheme was of human devising and, therefore, necessarily open to imperfection. After his defection from the ranks of the Nonjurors, Sherlock used this very argument in support of his own assertion, that a *de facto* King must be acknowledged once he is established, whether he has legal right or not; in other words that authority goes with possession regardless of established traditions of primogeniture.[1] Kettlewell stated the loyal High Church reply in his *Duty of Allegiance Settled Upon its True Grounds,*

[1] In his *Case of Allegiance Due to Sovereign Powers.*

where he wrote that God's "way of empowering the person must not be tied to revelation and particular nomination," but in the absence of revelation legal right is the best right, for God works through human institutions, of which law is one. Nor did he omit to point out that, failing human law on this point, the way is open for any usurper or faction to claim supreme authority, and ultimately the denial of law destroys the moral obligation of right altogether. "Providential possession," which was Sherlock's case, shows not right but fact, and only supposes a right—"its business is only to accomplish events, not to justify or authorize them or the actors in them."[1] To a man of Kettlewell's temper, indeed to any Nonjuror, there could be no valid argument against Right, and indefeasible hereditary succession copied from God's ordinance, and ratified by English law and custom, was instinct with this essential quality of Rightness.

3. *The End of Government.*

In the almost complete absence of serious consideration of the true end or aim of government, it must be presumed that the Nonjurors reacted against the teleological views of their Whig opponents, and adopted the extreme Tory position of defence of the *status quo*. The Low Church Party, anxious to justify their attitude to the Revolution, and even more anxious to avoid the logical working out of the contract theory to its utilitarian conclusion, avoided

[1] *Duty of Allegiance*, Chapter V.

the horns of their dilemma by talking vaguely of the Public Good. Samuel Grascome alone among the prominent Nonjuring theorists took up the challenge and attacked the indefiniteness of their position. " Public good as a common noise or solitary plea," he wrote, "is never to be admitted without such criterions and other evidences accompanying it as may make it appear that what is pleaded is real."[1] Any pretence of reform must stand two tests, a civil test of conformity to the standard of the Constitution, and a religious test by the standard of the Gospel and the rules of righteousness. It involves asking whether religion be better secured ? Whether men's lives and properties are more safe ? And how are we to increase in strength, trade and riches ? He admitted that the maintenance of public good was a duty of the Government, but pointed out not only the difficulty of deciding in what such good really lay when every section of the community desired its fancied good to prevail, but also the danger that in attempting to achieve such good unlawful and dishonest means were not infrequently employed, to the ultimate moral detriment of the State. " I know not better how to compare the public good of a community than to the safety of a human body, when every part and member is right, sound and well-disposed and out of danger,"[2] wrote Grascome, nevertheless " in some cases particular persons or parties may, and must, suffer for the preservation of

[1] *A Reply to a Vindication of a Discourse* 1691, p. 26. (Vindication by Hill, of Stillingfleet.)
[2] *Ibid*, p. 25.

the community." But he did not follow up this examination by the definition of any public or social good towards which he himself desired governmental activities to tend.

A negative attitude distinguishes all Nonjuring writings on this point. It was generally assumed that the interests of the supreme ruler would coincide with those of his subjects, but those interests are not precisely defined. Even Kettlewell, whose theory of rights suggests that he might have made some positive contribution to a discussion on the aims of government, does not appear to have considered the question seriously. Charles Leslie, with possibly a tinge of cynicism, declared that " the end of government is to put an end to debates,"[1] and " to save us from the coercion of one another."[2] Elsewhere he drew a distinction between the repressive activities of government, and its positive object, noticing that the punishment of transgressors must be supplemented by the establishment of order and regularity, but he did not work out the general statement in the sphere of detailed application. Hickes went so far as to express complete amazement at the thought that the interest of the people or public good could be seriously preferred to that of a single individual who reigned as God's vicegerent, declaring that no government could ever be safe under such a principle. Minorities would always claim the right to resist, the deposing power would inevitably follow, and an eternal opposition would put an end to security and peace.

[1] *Rehearsal*, III, 17.   [2] *Ibid*, I, 158.

4. *The Origin of Society and Government.*

In strong contrast to this neglect of ends, the Nonjurors were nowhere more emphatic and definite than in their dealings with the origins of society and government. While all adopt the patriarchal theory which Filmer and others had put into such a prominent place in Anglican thought, Leslie's treatment of it is the most lucid and detailed. He based his arguments wholly on the Old Testament narrative, but approached his material with a more analytical mind than did some of his fellow-thinkers. The foundation upon which he built his theory is in the sentence, "A family is a little Kingdom, and a Kingdom is nothing but a great family."[1] He realized that primitive kingship had a social and not a geographical significance, and that in primitive times, when there was more than enough land to support each family without intensive cultivation, the earliest nations were wandering tribes with no territorial dominion. But implicit in the very nature of the family is the magisterial function of its head Generation in itself involves government. Adam, besides being the first father, was also the first king; he " was king and supreme civil governor as well as father. But because the first King was Father of all his subjects, and they who succeeded him did succeed to his authority, therefore Kings were called fathers of their country, and Father became a name to express authority." "Nature dictates pre-eminence to the elder, but God determines it in

---

[1] *A Battle Royal Between Three Cocks of the Game*, p. 128.

express words, Genesis iv. 7."[1] Without this patriarchal or magisterial rule a number of people, however great, would not be a society in any sense, for government is the essence of society. "It is government alone that can form men into society," wrote Leslie, "without it they are but a loose company of people, be they never so many, like a flock of sheep or a company of birds flying in the air,"[2] and again, "that which makes a Society is the charter by which they are incorporated, and the common rules by which they are governed."[3]

But Leslie was above everything anxious to prove the orthodoxy of his position, and in the *Best of All*, he declared that, far from claiming any originality, he is but asserting the official doctrine of the Church of England, as set forth in the famous *Convocation Book* of Bishop Overall. In accordance with this, the acts of Nature are not in themselves sufficient evidence to form a true picture of the first kingdom, so much so, that he described the creation of Adam himself as "A little out of the ordinary course of things," and due to a miraculous intervention on the part of God in the natural sequence of events. "I now tell you, that though the original of government, as I understand it, was pursuant to the dictates of Nature, yet I place it not altogether there, but chiefly in the positive institutions of God, which renders it clear and indisputable."[4] "The wisdom of God saw that the people are the worst

[1] *Best of All, Being the Students' Thanks to Mr. Hoadly*, p. 23.
[2] *The Second Part of the Wolf Stripped*, and *Rehearsal*, I, 178.
[3] *Rehearsal*, I, 82.
[4] *Best of All*, p. 20.

MONARCHICAL GOVERNMENT 65

judges of their own good, and that to give them liberty would be to their destruction. Therefore he appointed government among mankind."[1]

Though confessing that in his day, owing to sundry wicked persecutions, no contemporary reigning king could trace his descent directly back to Noah, Leslie was at some pains to demonstrate that patriarchal government as an institution had never been interrupted "from the time of Adam to the German Emperor." One ruler succeeds immediately to another; "like a ball perpetually tossed betwixt rackets, this ball of government was never yet let fall to the ground."[2] Not only does the King never die, but dissolution of government itself is a "whim and a dream." In order to account for the separation of the various branches of the Jewish race, Leslie had recourse once more to the Old Testament. "This division of nations was not brought to pass gradually in a long tract of time and in several ages as people multiplied and spread over the earth, but it was one act done at one time by that most astonishing miracle of the division of tongues, which did distinguish the nations."[3] Had the keenness of Leslie's forward vision been of as fine a quality as the loyalty with which he held to his view of ancient origins, he might have been one of the great creative minds in English political thought.

Grascome's conception of society as a body, while introducing the germinal idea of its evolutionary

---

[1] Supplement to *The New Association*, Part II, p. 6.
[2] *Ibid.*
[3] *Cassandra (But I Hope Not)*, p. 18.

growth as opposed to sudden and miraculous acts of intervention on the part of a God external to it, did not really mark any departure from the patriarchal theory of government, because he laid stress on the fact of the body's subjection to the dominance of the head.

5. *The Case Against the Contract.*

The emphasis which all Nonjurors laid upon their doctrine of origins was an integral part of their unflinching opposition to a Whiggism which based its own theories on the contractual State. The dispute between those who placed the ultimate sovereignty in the people and those who rigidly upheld the royal claim thereto was of course of long standing. It had been decided once in 1648, but the Restoration had apparently rescinded the verdict. The controversy which raged around the Exclusion Bills had revived it with renewed fierceness. The events of 1688 provided an even more severe test of faith by introducing once again the argument of hard fact into the maze of speculation.

A sermon preached by George Hickes before the Artillery Company of London, when he was a Royal chaplain, as far back as 1682, contained the gist of the pre-revolution case against the principle of popular sovereignty. Hickes was typical of those who at the time of the Revolution did not permit hard facts to obscure their vision or distort their conscience; he would have retracted no word of his sermon; he may well have preached many like it to the Nonjuring congregations after his deprivation. His respect for history forbade him to deny that in some known instances the people had been self-governing, and that obedience was due to them, or to their delegates who administered government, as in any other case. " I deny not," said Hickes, " but that God by His providence may invest the sovereign power in the body of the people, as formerly in Athens and now in the Cantons of Switzerland, and that, as formerly in Sparta, they may commit the exercise of it into a single person under the character of a King; but then such Kings are only equivocal kings, kings in name, but in reality subjects, and have the people for their sovereign lord who in these unhappy governments . . . are indeed the Ministers of God, and ought to be obeyed not only for wrath but for conscience' sake." The difficulty which this picture presented to the minds of Hickes and his fellow believers was not that of conceiving of such a State to exist at any given moment in time, but of tracing its history, of imagining how it had come into being, and how it could ever maintain itself in equilibrium. A front elevation view might display the peak of its prosperity, but a cross section could reveal nothing but strife and chaos. The impossibility of the existence of any historical document containing the original contract was not a serious point in the controversy. The fact of its non-existence might be flung as a taunt, but it was irrelevant to the main issue. Supposing there had ever been a contract, even if it were now irretrievably lost, how could it ever have come into being in the way in which the Whigs assumed? Hickes reviewed the impossibilities of the hypothesis, as so many of his party were to do after him. How, he asked, was the first assembly convened? Who decided on the original franchise? Did it include men only, or women and men? If there were any disqualifications on what basis were they founded? And by whom? Who presided? And in any assembly did the supreme power rest in the numerical majority or in superior wisdom? And did their acts bind absentees and the minority?

The contract theory, if taken literally, bristles with difficulties impossible of resolution, but these doubts concerning the birth of the contractual State are not the only problems which it presents. "If the sovereign power be radically and fundamentally seated in the people," declared Hickes, "then there is but one sort of sovereign government in the world, *viz.*, Democracy, and, by consequence, all other sovereigns, whether senates or princes, are usurpers and ought to be reduced or deposed."[1] But Democracy was not part of God's plan for the world, as that plan was revealed in the Old Testament, therefore it was self-condemned. *Vox populi* could never be *Vox Dei* to men accustomed to regard the sacred books of the Jews as containing the only revelation of divine providence. And not only was democratic government not mentioned in Jewish history; it was in direct opposition to that kind of government which God had originally set up when he

[1] *A Discourse of the Sovereign Power* (sermon before the Artillery Co.).

made Adam King. "You will easily perceive the excellency of the Scriptural hypothesis. It is free from all the afore-mentioned difficulties and absurdities ; it is more agreeable to the original of mankind from one single created father ; it leaves not so many pretences for sedition and rebellion ; it lays the highest obligations that can be upon the conscience of the sovereign to rule well. In a word, it is not only the most religious, but the most rational, easy and complete account of government to say that Sovereign States and Princes are God's ministers and not the people's, that they derive power from Heaven and not from men, and particularly that they have the power of the sword not by donation from the people but by the ordinance of God."[1] The opinion which makes so-called sovereign princes nothing more than trustees of the people, " with whom they have a virtual contract," so that " if they do not perform their trust by not using their power to the ends for which they received it, or abuse it to contrary ends, then they forfeit the power and authority with which they were entrusted by them,"[2] was one which all upholders of Divine Right were pledged to combat. It was inseparable in their minds from the thought of sedition, treason, rebellion, and that breakdown of all government which resolves society into anarchy and chaos. It was hated as the badge of Papacy, owing to its connection with the Pope's claim to the deposing

---

[1] *A Discourse of the Sovereign Power* (sermon before the Artillery Co.).
[2] *Ibid.*

power; it was hated more for the dire results which were accounted its inevitable legacy; and it was hated most of all for its unorthodoxy and flagrant disregard of the revealed will of God.

Jeremy Collier, writing after the Revolution was an accomplished fact, was concerned less with examples from Scripture than those from English history. He demonstrated that "The Kings of England hold their crown by right of conquest and succession, and consequently are no trustees of the people," therefore " the liberties of the subject are not founded upon the reservations of an original contract, for conquered peoples must not pretend to make their own terms."[1] Subjection, even if founded on consent, is on a forced consent, hence the ruler, as the ultimate wielder of force, could not himself be subject to dethronement. Further, the law of Nature demands the keeping of contracts, so that it is of their essence that they should be irrevocable. The multitude, according to Collier, is " as unstable as the wind," and liberty of resistance for which the contract theory stood, must be the worst security for peace and prosperity imaginable, owing to the irresponsible reaction of a crowd to half-fledged rumours.

Kettlewell discussed the Contract, as did Collier, not on its own merits, but in connection with its bearing on the problem of passive obedience. He observed that in the last resort advocates of resistance were compelled to fall back upon the Contract as the only basis upon which the subject could claim the

[1] *Vindiciae Juris Regii.*

right to oppose the sovereign. He acknowledged that " this Contract will not be pretended to be anywhere extant upon public record,"[1] but the existence of a written agreement was immaterial for the Contract itself was a redundancy. " Common reason and nature of Government give equal provision to all, and as much original contract to the subjects of absolute emperors as to those of legal monarchs, who, whatever liberties and provisions they have more, have them not from common reason, but the special limitations of their own laws."[2] A subject whose liberties are secured to him by the law of the land has no need to invent a contract for the easier achievement or better preservation of what is already his.

The relation between the supposed contract and law was further developed, though in a different direction, by Leslie when he pointed out that the liberties claimed by subjects as due to them in return for surrender of certain rights to the supreme governor were not, and could never be, anything but concessions granted by grace of the king. These so-called original rights guaranteed by law were neither original nor a part of the contract, for kings were the sole authors of law, and therefore existed prior to its formulation and might indeed revoke it at will. The people could only play the part of grateful recipients to the king's lead of gracious donor ; there was no rôle of bargainer cast for either side. Although Leslie was at least as quick as the rest of

[1] *Christianity a Doctrine of the Cross*, Chapter VII.
[2] *Ibid.*

his party to challenge his opponents to explain away the difficulties of their position in view of the problems of representation, franchise, minorities and so forth, his most valuable contribution to the discussion arose out of his own peculiar and profound religious idealism, and was a vital part of his whole theory of sovereignty.

The reality of God and the beneficence of his dealings with man was the axis around which Leslie's thought revolved. He conceived God to be firstly the ultimate and infinite source of all power and dominion, and, secondly, the dispenser of this power among man according to his own design manifest in the story of creation and all subsequent history. There was in this philosophy no room for any political contract; for, on the one hand, the people could not renounce that power which was not theirs to give, and, on the other, the patriarchal origins of government were so certainly demonstrated in history as absolutely to preclude any possibility of that pre-governmental state of nature out of which the contract was said to have arisen.

It was the fundamental axiom of Leslie's political faith that " Every government has absolute power over the lives as well as the estates of all their subjects without asking their leave or making any contract with them. They are born in subjection without conditions."[1] But no man can dispose of his own life as he will, because life is only in the power of God; therefore no man can give up to the Magistrate that which is not his, namely, this absolute power of

[1] *Best Answer Ever Was Made*, p. 21.

life and death. "If, as Mr. Locke says, and says he has proved it," wrote Leslie in *The Rehearsal*,[1] "No man can subject himself to the arbitrary power of another, no man can subject himself to any Government of what sort or size soever. Nor can there be such a thing as government kept up in the world. . . . And if, as he says again, 'no man can transfer to another more power than he has in himself,' and that 'nobody has power over in himself to destroy his own life,' then how came any government to have the power of life and death? Mr. Locke confesses the individuals could not give it. And who else was there to give it? I doubt a little Divine Right must come in here. What else can give to another that power over my life which I have not myself?" Divine Right was to Leslie, as to the rest of the Nonjurors, the only possible obligation upon the conscience of the citizen to submit to any government, and without any obligation of conscience nothing remains to maintain the relationship between ruler and subject except force, and there is an end of all morality. "There is no such thing as right or wrong, as just or unjust, nor can there be any settlement of government till we come to a Divine Right. To what else should I give up my life or my liberty if I can preserve them?"[2] The whole *raison d'être* of the Nonjurors was to witness to the reality of moral obligation in public life. Force might be the method of expediency, but expediency could never take precedence of conscience. The deprivations and subsequent ignominy which they

[1] *Rehearsal*, I, 38.   [2] *Cassandra (But I Hope Not)*.

endured at the hands of a government which their fellow countrymen thought expedient to set up, were proofs in themselves that their principles were no mere academic speculations, but were vital convictions capable of survival even under persecution.

Although Leslie attacked the conception of a pre-governmental state of nature with all his customary brilliance and thoroughness, he contrived to leave the impression that this alone of all the political doctrines upon which he expended the energies of his mind failed to produce in him a sense of reality. He wielded the lance of satire and manœuvred the artillery of reason, but he knew all the time that what he fought was a mirage, and there are signs of evident exasperation at the futility of the attack. "One would think these men had never read the first three chapters of Genesis,"[1] was his impatient protest, and the tone suggests that men so sublimely ignorant were outside the pale of rational argument.

It is not surprising that Leslie failed to treat Locke's reasoning very seriously, when he referred to the latter's treatises as "two (very trifling) discourses of Government . . . so admired by the Whigs."[2] " As there never was such an independent state of mankind as Locke or the rest of our popular orators vainly fancy," said Countryman to his Observator, "so cannot mankind fall into such a state more than the world into its original chaos. And if mankind were in such a state, they could no more produce government from the consent of every individual than the chaos, by its own natural force,

[1] *Best of All*, p. 22.   [2] *Ibid*.

could have produced this world by a fortuitous concourse of atoms."[1] But this criticism was levelled by Leslie, not so much at Locke's state of nature, which gave men the right to private property before they consented to create government, as at that described by Hobbes. The former might be discounted by two simple arguments—firstly, that tacit consent to government (which would be necessarily required by all citizens other than those who actively participated at all stages in the making of the original contract) presupposes the existence of government to consent to, and is therefore not its foundation; and secondly, that the idea that civil government is necessary in order to co-ordinate men's desires and make them mutually compatible involves consideration of the good of others, and thus at any moment may nullify the original foundation of the contract which was supposed to be self-preservation. Locke's double process contract invents society to preserve life, and then sets up government to hang men who fight for their rights.

Towards the Hobbesian state of nature, Leslie turned the weapon of his satire. "Hell itself," he declared, "could not subsist without government," and he undertook to describe for the benefit of Benjamin Hoadly, whom he set up as *advocatus diaboli*, the country in which this celebrated Bishop sought for the origin of government. "Its name," he wrote, "is Chaos, and [it is] situated out of creation, which it complains of as an encroachment on its territories. The inhabitants are pre-Adamites, for

[1] *Rehearsal*, I, 38.

there are none other without Government. They have all one name, which is Ana, and everyone is King, whence their government (for they also have a shadow of it) is called Anarchy. They worship two idols, one is called Belial, the God of Liberty, and other, Beelzebub, the God of Flies . . . their tumultuous buzz is called the voice of the People."[1] And that was in itself, for Leslie, sufficient condemnation of the contract theory. To a man who believed as sincerely as he did in the divine nature of sovereignty and the divine origin of government, there could be nothing but unreasonable sin and treason against God in a theory which made government on organization arising from the exercises of the human will, and vested authority in a multitude of the common people.

[1] *Best Answer Ever Was Made*, pp. 27-28.

CHAPTER IV

SOVEREIGNTY

1. *Source and Nature of Authority.*

To the Nonjurors the problem of Authority, not less than that of origins, was primarily a religious one. Authority was regarded as being, as it were, incarnate in the person of the supreme ruler, and to a diminishing degree in his ministers and servants down to the humblest father in the kingdom; but it was itself a moral quality, a gift derivable from no other source than God himself. It followed from this that the secular State, whether it acknowledged itself to be so or not, was in the last resort a theocracy; that, God being omnipotent, right must in the long run prevail even against might; and that resistance to rightful authority involved in every case the offering of resistance to God. The only legitimate attitude for the ordinary citizen was that of obedience to his superior. He might on occasion be invited to choose someone as his representative in Parliament, or to take part in the election of some small *ad hoc* body to which might be entrusted some department of local government. But without specific invitation he had no right to any share in government at all, and even acting by it he had no direct legislative power, for laws were less than nothing until the King's seal was upon them; they derived validity solely from the royal authority.

Such a system might serve well enough as the philosophical background of a static and homogenous society. Once the door is opened to the explosive power of scepticism, once the suspicion of a dual control is aroused, or once a minority becomes strong enough or established power weak enough to threaten the omnipotence of the central government, then the conception of authority as a moral quality is apt to lose ground before the idea of force. Then, too, in the minds of politicians, the Divine Right of Kings varies in inverse ratio to the natural rights of the common people, and while obedience may still be regarded as the paramount political virtue, the authority to whom it is due may undergo a change of form far more profound than any change of mere personnel.

The position occupied by the Nonjurors in the political landslide of the Revolution, then, was that of defenders of the old order against the new, of right against might, of the ultimate sovereignty of God against the claim that sovereignty was vested in the body of the people. They in their turn made the counter-claim that nothing but allegiance to a divine authority could in the long run ensure the continuation of loyalty to the secular state.

In the English constitution the supreme sovereignty, under God, was vested in the King; that is to say that the " last resort " of government was to be found in him. The ultimate sovereign

SOVEREIGNTY

was, however, said to possess certain inalienable rights which were inherent in its abstract nature regardless of the concrete form through which it acted in society. Hickes, in his *Jovian*, gave a definition of them : " By the rights of the Sovereign I understand those prerogatives and pre-eminences of Power and greatness which are involved in the formal conception of sovereignty, and are inseparably annexed to the sovereign, whether it be the people, as in democracies, or a few of the chief, as in aristocracies, or one single person, as in monarchies. For there are certain essential rights of sovereignty or supremacy which equally belong to sovereigns of all sorts, and which without destroying the very notion of a sovereign you cannot abstract from him, no more than roundness from a circle or a sphere. For they constitute the essential difference between supremacy and subjection, so that whosoever hath them is a complete sovereign, and whosoever wants them, or any of them, is a subject, or at least an incomplete sovereign, and in all perfect and regular governments these essential rights of sovereignty equally belong to the supreme power, whether princes or states, by the common or statute laws thereof."
These Rights are :

(1) " To be accountable to none but God."
(2) " To have the sole power and disposal of the sword."
(3) " To be free from all coercive power."
(4) " Not to be resisted or withstood by force upon any pretence whatsoever."

(5) "To have the legislative power, or the power that makes any form of words a law."[1]

Apart from Leslie[2] the fullest exponent of the theory of Authority current among the Nonjurors was Kettlewell. He was above all things a believer in the divine overruling of the affairs of men. To the question "Doth God exercise over the world a sovereign Empire?" he returned an unqualified affirmative, adding, "all other rulers are but his ministers, but he still keeps the controlling power and the reins of government in his own hands."[3] Elsewhere he stated that "all loyalty to the King must consist with true religion towards God, since the King is only God's vicegerent."[4] Hence to him all problems of authority and allegiance were necessarily viewed in the setting of an ultimate theocracy, all right was divine right, and politics were inseparable from religion. In his *Duty of Allegiance Settled upon its True Ground*, which was a reply written in 1691 to Sherlock's *Case of Allegiance Due to Sovereign Powers*, Kettlewell not only replied point by point to the Dean's vindication of his action in taking the oaths, but gave a clear account of the nature, source, and purpose of authority as he saw them. He made civil authority a two-edged instrument when he defined it as "Right or Liberty in one to order or do a thing in civil matters, laying an obligation on

[1] *Jovian*, Chapter X.
[2] Leslie's views on Sovereignty and Church-State relationships, etc., are separately considered in Chapter VI.
[3] *The Practical Believer*, Part I, Chapter III.
[4] *A Sermon Intituled the Religious Loyalist*.

others to follow or submit to him."[1] The cornerstone of the whole position is the word "Right," involving as it does the sense of moral significance. An internal bond of obligation binding the subject to the sovereign is the essential property of authority irrespective of whether the authority is able to use force to ensure it or not. The power of the sword, which belongs to the supreme sovereign, is an external means of enforcing his authority and not the authority itself, for the one is a bodily instrument and the other is a moral and insubstantial quality. Although it was necessary in the circumstances to emphasize this quality of rightness as the only essential criterion of authority rather than to insist on the coercive power of the sword, Kettlewell was careful to enumerate several historical examples (which he knew his opponents could not repudiate), showing that, far from being an *ad hoc* doctrine, this distinction between right and power was an accepted tenet in Anglican theory. King Charles I., for instance, was held to have been still possessed of his authority even at the moment when he was a prisoner under sentence of death; his son, too, was invested with all regal authority immediately on the execution of the King, though for years he was prevented from exercising any ruling power over his subjects.

With such examples it was difficult indeed to account for the denial which Sherlock and the other Jurors made of James II.'s authority, even though he, too, was an exile. Kettlewell argued that " 'tis

[1] *Duty of Allegiance*, Chapter II.

a great blow to have the head of the State kept from communication with the body, but this does not dissolve the being of the Society, for that lies in the mutual relation and obligation of the Head and members,"[1] and such obligation stood unrepealed. To say, as Sherlock had said, that William became invested with the authority of a King simply because he acquired the power of one, was to mistake altogether the nature of authority by substituting its attribute for its essence. "It seems very strange," as Kettlewell pointed out, "that forcible possession should be a title to authority which cannot be forcibly possessed."[2] To say further, that William received his authority from the Convention representing the English people, was equally strange, and moreover was verging on blasphemy, for it was to assert that the people were capable of giving that which, in fact, was at the sole disposal of God. If it be true that "A human act must place a person in the State," it is only a half-truth, the complement of which is that "then the law of God vests him with God's authority to act therein."[3] The human choice of a King needs the specific grant of Authority by God in order to ratify the appointment, "and this is not to fetch the Authority of Kings or other superiors from the people . . . for the Authority is God's authority, not the people's, and that which carries the authority is God's own command."[4]

Human right of choice is exercised either through law, such as the law of entail, or by submission,

---

[1] *Duty of Allegiance*, Chapter VIII. [3] *Ibid*, Chapter II.
[2] *Ibid*, Chapter V. [4] *Ibid*, Chapter II.

SOVEREIGNTY

which is consent, whether implied or expressed. "So long as people only consent to give up their own, not what is the right of a third person, such consent gives a human right,"[1] but no one can give away that which is not his own; therefore the subject can only give his submission if he has a right to it, which he manifestly has not, for it belongs to the *de jure* king who alone can transfer it. This did not lead Kettlewell into support of the Contract theory, as might appear at first sight, because, by definition, this submission of the subject which is the right and possession of the King, is inherent in the nature of Authority itself, and therefore is derived from God and not from the subject. Even from the statement, "when a King's person dies, his personal rights die with him," it does not follow that the subject is free to dispose of his obedience on the death of a king, for the interval between the death of one king and the accession of another is as unreal as the moment of time between to-day and to-morrow, and the submission belongs instantly to the new king.

The obvious difficulty of deciding on any sure and certain test which would demonstrate irrefutably the right of any man's title to Authority, was one which greatly exercised the mind of Kettlewell. In the absence of any particular nomination, it was presumed that God would work through human laws and respect custom which had become embodied in them. "To think of Authority coming to anyone without good title of Right thereto, neither agrees, I think, with the nature of things as Right and

[1] *Duty of Allegiance*, Chapter IV.

Authority, or with the purpose of him who is to have it, nor with the honour and justice of God who is to give it, nor with the meaning and obligation of the commandment, which is to carry and convey this Authority from God to the person authorized."[1] Yet it was not to be supposed that God was tied by human laws. The whole discussion on this point is reminiscent of the attitude of mind crystallized in the adage, "Trust in God and keep your powder dry." God works through men who do their duty rather than those who ignore it or go contrary to it. If the nation is vigilant to keep the laws and flee revolutionary tendencies, then God, the first source of all authority, will see to it that right will prevail. In times of doubt the human conscience must be accepted as the final guide, backed by such knowledge as is available to the ordinary citizen, and it is no excuse to say that the conscience is too frail to bear the burden of responsibility for it should be kept fit and virile through exercise in the everyday affairs of life. After all, as Kettlewell pointed out, the onus of proof was at least as heavy on the side of his opponents. If Sherlock's assertion that allegiance was due to any "settled government" meant anything at all, it would have involved him and the whole Anglican Church in the acknowledgment that the Rump had been the rightful and authoritative government in its own day, for the power of the Rump had been exercised for a much longer period than that of William's kingship by the year 1691. But to acknowledge the Rump was a step which even

[1] *Duty of Allegiance*, Chapter III.

Sherlock was not prepared to take, though the reasons he gave in his *Case of Allegiance* to disprove the accusation, were, to say the least, more picturesque than convincing.

Kettlewell asserted that the purposes of Authority are to claim obedience and to ensure the exclusive rights of property. Property was to him an effect inseparable from right, even though possession might not be assured. If he intended the reference to be to material property, to say, as he did, that " the unjust possessor gets no property " was hardly a statement of literal fact, for a thief may obviously acquire property even while he lacks the right to it. It is more probable that he was concerned only with property in the sense of the possession of the moral quality of Authority, for he went on to re-affirm the connection between Right and Authority. " Take away Right from Authority and then Authority in that person is neither to be defended or obeyed."[1] If an usurper claiming Authority can offer no proof of it save that he won it by force of arms, then that in itself argues against his possession of it, for it cannot be acquired by such means. " If one wants it, mere strength can never give it, and if one has it, mere lack of strength can never lose it."[2]

Finally, this Authority is always personal. Obedience is not due to the administration of government where that is divorced from the rightful governor, and it is due to misused Authority where it is owing to the misuser. Power always resides in a person, and even the abuse of power cannot absolve

[1] *Duty of Allegiance*, Chapter III.   [2] *Ibid.*

the subjects from that personal relationship of submission in which God has placed them, when in one single act he granted Authority to the supreme governor, and ordained the obedience of all the governed.

This question of the personal nature of authority was naturally one to which the Nonjurors gave considerable prominence, for if obedience was due to the exercise of sovereignty irrespective of the person or persons in whom the sovereignty was rightfully invested, then there need have been no new political cleavage after the revolution. All could, as Sherlock had done on second thoughts, have acknowledged the new government which was obviously *exercising* authority, even if they had found it a duty to protest against the initial transference of power from James to William on the score of the moral inalienability of James' rights. Collier, writing in 1689, declared that " with us the King and only he, is the irresistible power ; neither must the prerogative be restrained to his person, but extend to his authority."[1] Hence all the King's ministers and lesser magistrates were to be regarded as representing the King's person when they acted as his deputies in the exercise of his authority, and in that capacity they were never to be resisted by force, though they were accountable to law in a sense in which the King was not. He further explained that the law forbidding resistance to those commissioned by the King " was designed to combat that pernicious distinction between the King's *Person* and

[1] *Vindiciae Juris Regii.*

his *Authority* . . . though in reality it is nothing but the King's authority which makes his person sacred."[1]

It was the tragedy of the Nonjurors that in their unswerving devotion to the moral obligation of conscience as a political motive they were called upon to make their sacrifice in a cause so unworthy as that of James II. But at least they were not dazzled by a principle to an extent sufficient to blind them to fact. They never pretended that their King was infallible, and would have been thankful enough to have served a master more worthy of their devotion. Whatever they thought of James as a man, however, they were in no shadow of doubt concerning their attitude towards him as a King. His power was from above and was irresistible. Here was no room for any principle of trusteeship in any form. Hickes vehemently denounced the view that inferior magistrates were God's trustees to see that the Prince performed the duties of his office in a fit manner, as contrary to Scripture, history and reason, in that it would erect a dual authority fighting against itself, and render the execution of government impossible. On the other hand, equally heretical in the sight of Nonjurors was the theory that Kings were themselves trustees of the people. " It is flat nonsense," wrote Grascome, "to talk of any supreme governor if he be only a trustee or commissioner of the peoples ; and every man will pride himself as no less than a petty king while those who are supposed to be only intrusted with the Govern-

[1] *Vindiciae Juris Regii.*

ment are accountable to him and the rest of the original kinglings."[1]

2. *Authority and Law.*

The question of how the supreme authority was to be diffused throughout the nation so that the " right or liberty of one to order " might establish its claim over " the obligation on others . . . to submit," was the question of law. The law acts as a connecting link between sovereign and subject in a fashion comparable to that in which the trunk of a tree connects the root and the branches. The essence of sovereignty is transmitted through it and diffused to the utmost extremity of the state. By it the diverse elements of the many-branched community are held together in a common relationship to the root and foundation of their being. Without it they would cease to live ; through it they receive that sustenance which is the condition of life ; and by it the direction of their growth and development is determined. The simile may be pressed even a stage further. It is conceivable that a cutting of the tree may develop roots of its own and thereafter maintain an existence independent of the parent ; but it is quite beyond the bounds of possibility that life should persist in the organism as a whole, once the vital connection between it and its roots is severed. Without the roots there can be neither trunk nor branches ; without the sovereign, both law and community lose their meaning.

[1] *Schism Triumphant*, Introduction.

The political theories of a nation without a written Constitution, perhaps more than those of other nations, are built up by inductive processes. Precedents may be acted upon for many generations before they are allowed the status of laws. Whereas the Whigs who brought about the Revolution had to seek for a theory of origins which would provide a rational background for their progressive ordering of the affairs of the kingdom, the orthodox Tories would not allow that present necessities could justify any political action which would fail to harmonize with a predetermined order of events whose origins were revealed in Scripture. Hence the growing power of Parliament since the days of Charles I. was still, in the last decades of the seventeenth century, outside the range of vision of Anglican political orthodoxy, although such power had not infrequently ministered to Anglican political needs.

The orthodox view was that all laws derive their validity from the authority of God mediated through the person of the supreme sovereign in the State. When Hickes, therefore, defined legislative power as "the power that makes any form of words of law," he was only reiterating an accepted dogma of Anglo-Catholic political faith. But the inclusion of that definition in a list of the Rights of the Sovereign stiffened the attitude of mind which made it so difficult to reconcile that faith with the accepted practice of the day. The possibilities of arbitrariness revealed in it might be a matter for regret, but the risks attendant upon a system which would give legislative power to any body of citizens irrespective of the King, or even one which would divide the authority of legislation (which was by divine right the King's sole prerogative) were so infinitely dangerous that even a tyranny was to be preferred to a constitution which failed to acknowledge the absolute supremacy of the royal authority.

Hickes drew a distinction between what he called "Imperial laws," or those which "are in eternal force against the subject in defence of the sovereign, be he good or evil, just or unjust, Christian or Pagan, be what he will,"[1] and "Political laws" which are made to secure the rights of the subject. But his "Political laws" were in themselves only concessions of a sovereign, and the subject had no inherent right to clemency. Even in cases, as in England, where the "Imperial laws" were theoretically limited by the "Political laws," "a king . . . is nevertheless as complete a sovereign, and hath the sovereign power as fully and entirely within himself, as he who is at liberty to exercise his authority as he will . . . so limited sovereigns are as perfect and essential sovereigns as the purely arbitrary and despotic."[2]

Sherlock also adopted this rather doubtful distinction between the absolute and the limited monarch. "A limited Prince may break laws," he wrote in 1684, "but he can neither make nor repeal them, and therefore he can never alter the frame or constitution of the government, though he may at present interrupt the administration of it."[3] At that

[1] *Jovian*, Chapter X.
[2] *Ibid.*   [3] *Case of Resistance*, Chapter VI.

time, in the year previous to the accession of James II., Sherlock had as little desire as any of his fellow High Churchmen, to admit the power of the people as a limiting influence upon the monarchy. His unalterable " frame and constitution " contained no place for the self-expressed rights of a democratic people, and it is difficult to find in practice any great difference between a prince who is irresistible though limited, and one who is irresistible because absolute. " Law is nothing else but the public and declared will and command of the law-maker,"[1] was his definition, and no one who looked at political institutions from the angle from which Sherlock regarded them, ha the least doubt but that the only law-maker in th kingdom was the King, to whom alone God had specifically entrusted the legislative power.

It follows that the part taken by Parliament in the legislative process is never more than that of a subject. Its consultative function and authority to negative are not powers to be exercised on equal terms with the powers of the sovereign. Kettlewell expressed this distinction when he wrote: " Though the King is not absolute without rules in governing, nor alone without partners in legislation, yet is theirs only a subject's part, not a co-ordinate sovereign's; and he alone is supreme both in legislation and execution . . . for our law and Church, too, fixes all the sovereignty of the realm solely in the King."[2] The three estates of the realm derive their whole existence from the express authority of the King,

---

[1] *Case of Resistance*, Chapter VI.
[2] *Christianity a Doctrine of the Cross*, Chapter VI.

whose writ and summons is their only right to meet. They contribute nothing to the right of the King, but receive all from him.

On the relation of the subject to that aspect of the sovereign power which was expressed through the medium of Parliamentary enactments, as distinct from the wider relationship of subject and sovereign in the abstract, the Nonjurors had little to say. The subject's whole duty, in either case, could be summed up in the word "obedience." The imposition of laws from above left no room for any other attitude, nor for any reserves of interpretation. Both Collier and Kettlewell attempted to rationalize this obedience on other terms than those of the rights of the sovereign, by claiming that laws were for the protection of the subject. There are "boundaries of right," in Collier's phrase, whose existence is a better assurance that the Prince will protect one citizen from the illegal acts of another. The invasion of civil rights by a private person may be resisted by an appeal to law, and the decision of subordinate executive officers who administer the law may be disputed until the appeal is decided by the supreme governor. But against the Sovereign there can be no appeal, only submission. If laws designed to restrain arbitrariness fail to accomplish their object, then there is no human help left by which a subject may obtain redress.

3. *Authority and the Subject.*

The uncompromising claim on the part of the Sovereign over the obedience of the subject, which the

Nonjurors so insistently reiterated, was based on three main foundations. To resist the Sovereign, or to attempt in any way to coerce him was not only illegal, it was also inexpedient and irreligious. In his Preface to *The History of Passive Obedience Since the Reformation*, which was a collection of extracts from upwards of a hundred different sources illustrative of the Anglican theory of non-resistance, Collier claimed as the immortal glory of the Church of England that she alone, as opposed to the Papists on one hand, and the Dissenters on the other, had preached the eternal and unalterable doctrine of obedience to the Sovereign as it had been practised in the early Church.

Sherlock, in 1684, had epitomized the non-resisters' view when he wrote : " Both the laws of God and of our country command us not to resist, and if death, an illegal and unjust death follow upon that, I cannot help it, God and our country must answer for it."[1]

By the laws of the land the King had sole power of the sword, and was free from all coercion regardless of the end to which he employed the sword, or of any acts of his which might be contrary to the law. The divine power which gave to the sovereign this supreme authority to make law, had not at the same time given the subject leave to resist him if he exceeded his authority or failed to abide by the law of his own creation ; on the contrary, it added the gift of his subjects' absolute submission.

In *Christianity a Doctrine of the Cross*, Kettlewell examined the doctrine of non-resistance from many

---

[1] *The Case of Resistance of the Supreme Powers*, Chapter VI.

angles, and attempted to refute the pleas which his opponents used to justify the contrary practice. He was no violent controversialist, as Sherlock or Hickes, but his aruguments gained rather than lost in force from the very moderation of his tone. On the historical side he instanced the attitude of the early Church under the persecutions of the Roman emperors as a worthy example of passive obedience, for its members forbore to resist in defence of their legal status and liberties as citizens, no less than of their religious rights as Christians. Lest any doubts remained concerning the relevance of the illustration, he made specific reference to the laws by which the Church was established in the England of his own day. The Act of Uniformity had declared it to be unlawful upon any pretence whatsoever to take up arms against the King; the XXXIX Articles fixed the sole sovereignty of the realm in him; by the Oath of Supremacy the subject was bound to promise allegiance, and to defend all the jurisdictions, privileges and authorities belonging to the King or annexed to the Crown. On purely civil grounds the case was equally strong, for the Militia Acts of 13 and 14, Car. 2, denied utterly that either House of Parliament might make either defensive or offensive war against the King. The English Constitution was based on the sole sovereignty of the King, and his complete freedom from coercion; any thought of resistance against him was, therefore, altogether alien to it.

The impossibility of defining cases of extreme necessity, or of recognizing the point at which a breach of the fundamental laws of the nation becomes serious enough to warrant resistance, was, in Collier's view, adequate reason in itself for declaring all resistance to be equally illegal. But he also pointed out that English law added its express command to the subject to obey, and "if the authority of the kingdom declares their Prince irresistible, this makes him as much so as if he had given himself this power by conquest."[1] "The law," he wrote, "is certainly the measure of all civil right, and therefore to carve out ourselves a greater security than the law allows is destructive of all government.[2] No state can continue to exist if it allows its citizens any reserves of interpretation with regard to the law and constitution, for a law must have no exceptions apart from those which are explicit in its formulation. Collier, with what his enemies may have regarded as somewhat unwarranted optimism, declared further, that the Prince's own instinct of self-preservation would be sufficient to prevent him from trespassing on the civil rights of his subjects in any fashion prejudical to the country's good, and that, if he had assurances of peaceableness from his subjects, he would be encouraged to clemency. But the political situation in the England of 1689 made this argument hardly a safe weapon with which to defend his position, and Collier wisely laid a heavier emphasis on the argument from expediency.

The Civil Wars and subsequent events in England during the exile of Charles II. were still, after the space of less than half a century, fresh enough in the

[1] *Vindiciae Juris Regii.*   [2] *Ibid.*

mind of the Anglican Church to add colour to the belief that resistance of any sort offered to the Crown must inevitably bring disaster and chaos on the country. The loyal advocates of non-resistance were fully aware that their doctrine might lead to suffering on the part of individuals, or even of the whole Party. They accepted the risk and endured the penalties, being convinced that, whatever inconveniences the principle might bring in its train for them, these were far easier to be borne than those which would be, for the whole nation, the inevitable accompaniment of its opposite. In the one case, a tyrant might vent his excesses on particular persons or parties who alone would bear the brunt of his attack. But a tyrant could not in a year do as much damage as a mob in a week, and, once resistance was permitted, mob rule would prevail. " In civil war, which is worse than any tyranny, all must suffer without distinction, and however it may be called defensive and at first be so designed, yet it will certainly degenerate into offensive, and rapine, and bloodshed, and devastation will be the ordinary concomitants thereof."[1] Nor could the individual hope to gain any benefit from civil war in the long run, for it would bring about the dissolution of civil government, and once government was dissolved the laws upon which individual rights to title and estates rested were lost, too. Nothing could then remain to the private citizen save what he could get by force or fraud, and no superior authority would be in existence which could safeguard property thus acquired.

[1] Hickes, *Jovian*, Chapter XI.

Further, to resist the sovereign was inexpedient not only because it involved such disastrous consequences, but equally because as a method of achieving any desired good it was bound to be ineffectual. Admittedly, the only reasonable defence which could be advanced for a policy of deliberate resistance was that it was a means to the accomplishment of some end, the great value of which justified the temporary breaking of the salutary habit of non-resistance. The exigencies of human affairs might be said to demand, on rare occasions, the sacrifice of obedience, as a lesser virtue, on the altar of some greater public good, such as the preservation of religion. The reply of Nonjurors to this Machiavellian type of argument was straightforward and uncompromising. Archbishop Sancroft himself had never for a moment gone back on the condemnation of such reasoning, which he had pronounced over thirty years before the Revolution, when he described the true statesman as one who " is inviolably constant to his Principles of Virtue, and religious prudence ; his ends are noble, and the means he uses innocent ; he hath a single eye on the public good ; and if the ship of state miscarry, he had rather perish in the wreck than preserve himself upon the plank of an inglorious subterfuge . . . the star he looks to for direction is in Heaven, and the port he aims at is the joint welfare of Prince and People."[1] Those who were prepared in 1689 to " perish in the wreck " with him, were all equally

[1] *Modern Policies from Machiavel Borgia, and Other Choice Authors.*

convinced of the futility of offering resistance to the Sovereign in order to secure those moral gains which, in the nature of things, were not to be won by force. "There's no storming of a creed," wrote Collier, "if it's not betrayed by cowardice or treachery it is impregnable."[1]

If the creed were by its nature impregnable, then it was entirely unnecessary to elaborate defences for it, and an attempt to hold it by force would be as futile as an attempt to take it by similar methods. But even were such a defence necessary and feasible, that would not make it morally right. God, who in his wisdom gave to men both their religion and the courage wherewith to uphold it in face of persecution and tyranny, had never authorized them to protect it by force, or to withstand in ways contrary to his law those who sought to mutilate or destroy it.

But although the defence of the faith might be propounded as the chief motive for resistance, it was not the only one. If God's prohibition included the greater, it extended also over all lesser defections from the path of obedience, upon which he had set the feet of all subjects when he first endued sovereign kings with a measure of his own authority. Popular objections to the doctrine of non-resistance which might arise, in Sherlock's phrase, from "mere natural reason," could have no weight with the Nonjurors unless the commands of God could also be refuted; but they had little difficulty in demonstrating from Scripture and illustrating from the history of the Early Church that the plain and express

[1] *Vindiciae Juris Regii.*

SOVEREIGNTY 99

laws of God forbade resistance to the Sovereign in any circumstance. The rebellion of Korah against Moses was a fruitful example of the sin of resistance; the saying of Christ that men should " render unto Cæsar the things which are Cæsar's," and his command to Peter against the use of his sword in the Garden, were both used again and again to illustrate the duty of Christians towards their earthly Sovereign. St. Paul's assertion that " whosoever resisteth the higher power resisteth the ordinance of God, and they that resist shall receive to themselves damnation," was in itself sufficient to shape the opinion of any body of men deeply imbued with the Pauline version of Christianity. It was indeed difficult to imagine that anyone who accepted this theology could escape from the logic of the argument.

To attempt to palliate resistance on the grounds that the moral qualifications or the political acts of the Prince were evil was beside the point, for subjects were bound to him not as man, but only as the deputy of God to whom in all things must obedience be given. If the authority of the King, which was his title to the allegiance of his subjects, was, as the advocates of divine right maintained, solely derived from God, it was impossible to evade the conclusion that resistance offered to an earthly Sovereign was *ipso facto* directed towards the divine Ruler of the Universe himself. The presumption which inspired such resistance would certainly bring those who practised it to the Mosaic pit or the apocalyptic lake of fire.

Even so, as Collier, writing words of encouragement and admonition to his own Party, asserted, "rebellion is not the only damning sin, no more than plague is the only mortal distemper. If we are true to the king and false to God Almighty, if we keep the oath of allegiance and break that of baptism, if we decline solemn perjury and are guilty of common swearing, our case must be miserable hereafter."[1] The problem of divided allegiance was an ever-recurring one, and presented grave difficulties to men whose boast it was that they would rather die as martyrs than as rebels. To Kettlewell, who, perhaps more than any other Nonjuring political writer invariably gave the spiritual aspect of any situation paramountcy over the secular, the alternative of turning a "bigoted rebel" or "an irreligious time-server," which apparently confronted the Christian subject of a persecuting Prince, was one which called for serious consideration. In a sermon, preached within a short time of James II.'s accession he had said, "Sometimes Princes profess a wrong religion ; nay, sometimes they set themselves against the true and persecute God's servants. And when at any time this is the case, our duties to God and the King seem as if they were at odds, and look like irreconcilable and inconsistent things. And then men oftimes think themselves exempt from one of them, because they cannot serve two masters of contrary interests ; so that either in zeal for religion they cast off all duty to their Prince . . . or else in compliance with their Prince, they throw aside true religion. . . . But the true determination of the case

[1] *A Persuasive Consideration Tendered to the Royalists.*

SOVEREIGNTY

... is neither of these. When Princes happen to have any mispersuasions about religion, we must still pay them all civil subjection and obedience. But our loyalty must not carry us to embrace their errors, but at the same time we must keep true to religion and God's service."[1] If the Prince should command a thing unforbidden in Scripture, then his command would be lawful and " no good subject must dispute or question, but peaceably and readily perform." If his commands enjoin those things forbidden in Scripture, and therefore unlawful to be performed, and the subject cannot obtain exemption from obedience either by petition or other lawful means, then the case is helpless from a human point of view, and only God can redress it. A conscientious refusal to obey the Prince here may be forgiven hereafter, but rebellion against God merits eternal punishment.

Nevertheless, if active obedience to the Prince becomes inconsistent with duty towards God, the subject is not then freed from his political allegiance, but must convert active into passive obedience, which involves keeping under obedience to the sovereign powers even when suffering wrongfully at their hands. The religious rights of the subject, *i.e.*, the right to believe and do those things of which his conscience approves as acceptable to God, were the only ones which carried in their nature any possibility of exemption from active obedience, and such exemption as they offered was not the parent of liberty, but of submission.

[1] *The Sermon Intituled the Religious Loyalist.*

In spite of the seeming sternness of their doctrine of obedience, the Nonjurors were not regardless of the claims to natural and civil rights which civilized man customarily makes. It was acknowledged that the Sovereign required the allegiance of subjects rather than the subjection of slaves. Conditions which required of the subject anything but an active and willing obedience were abnormal. In the ordinary course of events the subject had ample security which guaranteed his enjoyment of the privileges of citizenship, without imposing upon him uncomfortable and unnecessary restraints.

Hickes discussed the problem at length in his *Jovian*, and though he denied that there could be any absolute security for either the Sovereign or the subject, he enumerated certain safeguards which in his opinion protected the latter against the former with as great a certainty as the doctrine of non-resistance protected the Prince. These were—firstly, the providence of God, who delights to give his children those good things which he sees will be for their benefit; secondly, the conscience of the Prince on whose mind the " common principles of humanity, justice and equity are engraven by the finger of God"; thirdly, the Prince's honour, which will prevent him from committing those acts which would blemish his reputation among neighbouring sovereign powers; and fourthly, the laws of the land and the courts of justice, the abolition or gross misuse of which, by the sovereign, would be of such extreme difficulty as to make it practically impossible.[1]

[1] *Jovian*, Chapter XII.

SOVEREIGNTY

Jovian was written before James II. had done his best to play havoc with the English Constitution, but the faith of the non-resisters was not to be shaken. Collier, in 1689, declared that " we have the Prince's honour, conscience and interest to secure us,"[1] and Kettlewell, two years later, was still able to write of the laws of the realm as " the only possible restraint of arbitrariness,"[2] a restraint which was all the more operative because in the nature of the case the ultimate Sovereign could not himself perform all the acts of state, and his ministers who deputized for him were accountable for any breach of the laws which they committed in the exercise of their office. Kettlewell, in fact, seems to have summed up the mind of his Party when he said " Government is the best safeguard of our liberties and properties. And if once we go to pull it down, we go at the same time . . . to pull down ourselves and to set upon our own freedoms. The fence being broken down, the inclosure becomes common, and our rights lie open to all intruders."[3]

It was not denied that the citizen had certain natural rights which were inherent in his manhood, most obvious of which was the right of self-defence against the attack of any private person. The man who, being in a state of nature, assumed an attitude of passive obedience towards a murderer would be a fool rather than a martyr; and a citizen who, in an emergency, found himself beyond the protection of civil

[1] *Vindiciae Juris Regii.*
[2] *Christianity a Doctrine of the Cross*, Chapter IX.
[3] *Ibid*, Chapter VII.

law, might be regarded for the time being as equally in his natural state, and thus at liberty to defend himself by whatever means lay at his disposal. But once these natural rights were incorporated into the civil code, and thus granted the status of civil rights and made defensible by law, the only true protection of them lay in taking legal measures.

In any case, the forcible defence of rights, whether natural or civil, was only applicable against private persons, and never in any circumstances against the Sovereign, to whose grace the civilizing of natural rights was ultimately due. It might be called "natural" that an inhabitant of a civilized state should claim certain privileges as his rights, but without an act of royal favour and condescension confirming the claim, the possession of them would be so precarious as to nullify any value with which they might be thought to endow their owner. Beggars cannot be choosers, and the liberties which the subject accepted as his due were, in fact, a pure donation by act of the sovereign grace, and as such had to be accepted on the Sovereign's terms. This concession theory of right, besides being used as an argument against resistance, also played an important part in determining the mutual relationship of Church and State.

CHAPTER V

CHURCH AND STATE

1 *Distinction between the Permanent and Occasional Aspects of the Problem.*

IF it be true that, as Lord Acton said, the solution of the problem of the relation between the spiritual and secular power " is among the objects and would be the end of all history,"[1] then the contribution brought by men whose experience was so intimately bound up in Church and State affairs as was that of the Nonjurors, must have peculiar relevance to any discussion of political thought. The sacrifice of men who were prepared to give up not only their career and reputation, but in some cases their sole means of livelihood, rather than deny either their political allegiance or the moral obligation which bound them to it, was a sacrifice made in order to witness to the absolute supremacy of spiritual authority over all other powers whatsoever. Whether the motive was one of fear, as it doubtless was in some cases, or of a genuine devotion to the practical application of religious principles as they saw them enshrined in the Church, is, in a sense, immaterial, for ultimately the thought of God lies behind both. Those whose

[1] *Political Thoughts on the Church*, 1858, reprinted in *The History of Freedom*.

vision was wide enough to see the controversies of temporal states in the setting of an eternal theocracy, and who were prepared to take tremendous risks on the assumption that what they saw was the truth, are entitled to respect as men of sincere, even if not always of tolerant, mind.

The holding of an implicit conviction regarding the fundamental reality of the spiritual power did not necessarily imply that all the politico-religious problems which forced themselves upon the attention of the Nonjurors were of equal permanent significance. There were, in fact, certain aspects of the controversy, which, arising out of the immediate events of the revolutionary period, were so coloured by them that they had little importance in subsequent history except in so far as they illustrated underlying principles. Thus the so-called "State point" concerning the oaths, and involving consideration of William's title to the throne, is, after a lapse of over two hundred years, important not in itself, but chiefly as indicating a belief in the necessity for religious sanctions obliging the subject to civil obedience. Similarly, the question of the "immoral prayers" has little direct connection with the main stream of political thought, although the underlying problem of the relation between the liturgy and the legislature is as much in evidence in the twentieth as in the seventeenth century. The whole controversy over the "Church point," or schism by the lay deprivations of the Nonjuring bishops and clergy, becomes a domestic issue for the Church alone, unless it is viewed in connection with the larger problem of the inalienability of spiritual power, which involves the question of the establishment of religion in an official sense, and hence of the status of all associations within the State.

2. *The Oaths.*

The Nonjurors were but carrying on the tradition of their Church when they insisted on the sacred inviolability of the oaths which they had taken to James II. A great preacher in the Anglican Church, when delivering a sermon before the Judges of the Kingston Assizes in 1681, had said that the necessity for oaths " is so great that human society can very hardly, if at all, subsist long without them ; government would many times be insecure." Again : " This obligation no man can violate but at the utmost peril of the judgment and vengeance of God, for every oath implies a curse upon ourselves in case of perjury . . . and this was always the sense of mankind concerning the obligation of oaths." He went on to define his terms : " It is perjury when a man promises upon oath to do that which it is unlawful for him to do, because this oath is contrary to a former obligation," and " all departure from the simplicity of an oath is a degree of perjury," an affront to God, and treason against society. Private security of life and fortune, no less than public peace and justice, are endangered by the man who is guilty of this most heinous sin.[1]

[1] *The Lawfulness and Obligation of Oaths*, John Tillotson, D.D., Dean of Canterbury.

It is scarcely credible that the preacher whose eloquence was responsible for the expression of these views on the oaths was none other than he who, ten years later, stepped into the see of Canterbury, made vacant by the deprivation of Archbishop Sancroft. But Tillotson, in spite of his fervour, was possibly unconscious of his seeming inconsistency. He had been foresighted enough to provide himself a loophole through which to escape. "He is guilty of perjury after the act," he told the learned Judges, "who, having a real intention when he swears to perform what he promiseth, yet afterwards neglects to do it. Not for want of power (for so long as that continueth the obligation ceaseth), but for want of will and due regard to his oath." If this constituted the orthodox position, the problem which faced all those public servants whose holding of office, in 1689, required of them the taking of the oaths of Allegiance and Supremacy, was to determine at what point the power to obey James passed out of their control. All the Anglican clergy were obliged to take the oath on ordination; how could they discover the precise conditions which, when they arose, would be such as to release them from their obligations?

Those who, like Tillotson, were satisfied in their consciences that the new oath to William did not involve them in perjury, based their reasoning on many and various grounds.[1] Questions of right, or

---

[1] This summary of arguments for the oath is taken from an anonymous pamphlet: *A Friendly Conference concerning the New Oath of Allegiance to K. William and Q. Mary wherein the objections against taking the oaths are impartially examined. And the reason for obedience confirmed from the writings of the*

legality of title to authority, they said, did not properly come within the purview of the subject. In English law the possession of the Crown was sufficient title to warrant a King's claim on the obedience of the citizens ; in any case, William did not (in 1689, at least) describe himself as rightful King—he left James' right to fend for itself, and did not profess to have acquired it. As there must be someone in supreme authority, it would be better for the well-being of the nation for subjects to acknowledge the *de facto* power regardless of whether it was *de jure* or not. Subjects must not criticize, but obey. In the event of the return of James, the English law would indemnify the subject who had sworn to obey William, which it would never do, in William's time, for those who refused so to swear. Obedience was due to William, not only out of gratitude to him for the preservation of the State, but also because a man owed it to himself, his family and his estate, to live peaceably and without offence, which he manifestly could not do if he refused the ordinance of the supreme authority. Not only so, but it might be presumed that the deposed Prince would have the true welfare of his people at heart, and would prefer that they should take all possible means, even including the oath of loyalty to the Prince in possession, to secure the execution of the laws, the defence of the realm, and the prosperity of trade —benefits which at the moment he was himself

profound Bp. Sanderson. And proved to agree to the Principles of the Church of England and the Laws of the Land, by a Divine of that Church, 1689.

unable to secure for them. To this end he would give his tacit consent to obedience to the usurper; otherwise he would not be seeking to further the best interests of his people, and would therefore be unworthy of their allegiance. Nor were the Jurors afraid of the doctrine of non-resistance; they merely applied it to the *de facto* King instead of to the *de jure*. They even suggested that those who desired the restoration of James would be justified in taking the oath to William, in order to save their lives, for they would be of more use to the Jacobite cause alive than dead. In any case, as active obedience to James was impossible, because the nation was ignorant of his commands, and passive obedience could do him no good, the obligation of the oath to him was dissolved, and its dissolution left the way open for the subject to take the new oath. Finally, "where the supreme Authority of the nation commands us anything that is not unlawful, as this oath of allegiance, we are not to consider the offences that private persons may take at it, but are to take heed lest we offend those that are in Authority."[1] The private person had no right to quit office in order to be saved the searing of his conscience caused by taking the oath, nor should he consider other men's opinions, but only his duty to the powers that be, for if every honest man refused office, all would be suspect, and their places would be filled by their enemies, who would thus gain control of both Church and State.

The casuistry of these arguments may have sufficed to persuade some to desert right and bow to might, if their material interests had not already

[1] *Friendly Conference*, p. 33.

done so, but it could have no influence on those for whom moral right was the mainspring of all their actions. If the choice lay, as apparently it did, should William push his authority to its logical limits, between being hanged in this world or damned in the next, the Nonjurors infinitely preferred the prospect of hanging. Moreover, they would rather have been hanged by an usurper for avoiding the damnable sin of perjury, than have suffered a similar disgrace at the hands of a restored *de jure* Prince for having acknowledged his rival, and so gone back on their principle of passive obedience as well as on their oath. A victim of the former end might not save his face, but would quite possibly preserve his soul, but he who risked the latter would most assuredly lose both. The oaths were sacred; considerations alike of personal safety in the temporal sense, or of so-called public good, were equally irrelevant. To ignore the oath taken to James by taking the new one to William would be perjury. Perjury was a damnable sin. There was nothing more to be said.

3. *Schism and Immoral Prayers.*

The Nonjurors were never more sincere than in their expression of the belief that they were the true Anglican Church, and that all the juring clergy and their flocks were in schism. They have been criticized on this point perhaps more than any other, but it is difficult if not impossible to escape the logic of their conclusions, if there be any truth in the premises on which they were based. There were, indeed, a few men who refused to take the oath of allegiance to William and Mary, but who continued in communion with those who did take it. The position which they adopted was a compromise which could hardly be justified by argument; for the Church to which they then belonged was built upon the foundations of resistance to the sovereign, and an acknowledgment of the validity of lay deprivations. But, as citizens, if they refused to take the oath to William, they could hardly be said to condone resistance to James; while, as clergy, if they recognized lay deprivation, they fell into an Erastianism which they professed utterly to repudiate.

But a charge of inconsistency is the last accusation which can be made against the great majority of Nonjurors. Just as it was impossible for them to acknowledge the usurper as King while the rightful King was still alive although unable to exercise his authority, so was it impossible for them to refuse recognition of the rightful bishops, even when the latter were excluded from the exercise of their true ecclesiastical function. A state deprivation might separate the bishops and clergy from the enjoyment of legal and civil privileges or financial support which were their right in an established Church, but the advantages of ecclesiastical establishment were not of the essence of the Church's being. The Church was a spiritual body whose life was derived from God. The trappings of incorporation with which it was clothed were from the State, and as such could be taken back by it, but the State could not withdraw that which was not in its power to give, and therefore could not affect that spiritual core of the Church's being which was of divine origin. Sancroft and the other Nonjuring bishops had in all points maintained the orthodox doctrine and practice of the Anglican Church. They had done nothing which merited canonical censure; a canonical censure was the only legal ground which could justify their deprivation. If such censure was not expressed—and nobody pretended that it was—there was absolutely no reason for supposing that their position as Fathers of the Church was altered by a hair's breadth. Indeed, in a phrase of one of their successors, to say that they had broken from the rest of the Church was as reasonable as to affirm that when a ship breaks from the shore where she is anchored the shore removes from her and not she from the shore.[1]

On the other hand, the Juring bishops had not only, as individuals, broken their oaths of allegiance to James, but had directly contravened the doctrine of their Church by allowing themselves to become involved in the processes whereby William had become King; for the 2nd Canon of the Church of England declared all those excommunicated *ipso facto* who did not own the King's authority, and by the King was understood he who was possessed of the throne according to the civil constitution of the English hereditary monarchy, *i.e.*, James II. Hence, as men guilty of perjury, or as Churchmen guilty of treason to their traditional doctrine, they were equally unworthy in the sight of their Anglo-Catholic

---

[1] Hickes, *An Apology for the New Separation, in a Letter to Dr. John Sharpe, Archbishop of York*, 1691.

brethren to carry on their spiritual mission. For men holding the Nonjuring position there was no alternative but to separate from the Revolution Church and to perpetuate their own communion by all means in their power.

The perpetuation of their Church led necessarily, as time passed, to the consecration of new bishops, but even before this necessity arose, the Nonjurors had become a distinct communion, owing to the organization of separate congregations for worship. Kettlewell put the case with his usual clarity: "When a second or opposite bishop is set up in any Church against a former orthodox one, who is still bishop thereof, the anti-bishop and they who set him up and adhere to him make the schism. For the other with his adherents as the same head and members abide still where they were, and are still the same Church."[1] Those who literally believed that the Jurors were not merely mistaken but flagrantly sinful, had no alternative but to break off communion with them, and the same reasons which to them justified such a break justified the habit of continuing separate meetings. The body of Christ was not tied to majorities; truth could abide in a minority and it was truth which constituted the Church a spiritual body and not certain buildings, or a State-appointed hierarchy or merely a large proportion of the religious population of the country. The preservation of unity in the Church, however cherished as an ideal, was of secondary

[1] *Of Christian Communion to be Kept in the Unity of Christ's Church*, Part III, Chapter I.

CHURCH AND STATE

importance when compared with the preservation of truth.

Even so, the difficulties attendant upon the circumstances of the Nonjurors as a community made it impossible for scattered members to keep in close or regular touch with congregations of their fellow-believers, and divergencies of practice arose. Kettlewell, for instance, was of those who believed that the maintenance of opportunities for all to partake of the ministrations of the Church was of paramount importance, and gave it as his opinion that, though "to avoid the guilt of schism, men are to disclaim and stand off from the communion of anti-bishops and not to participate in their ministrations, yet is that strictly on the supposal of room or opportunity to participate more regularly with others. But want of other ministrations will be an excuse for the faultiness of seeking them from them, and it will be allowed, I conceive, to take up therewith from schismatics rather than to live without any ministerial offices at all."[1] Hickes, as representing the more rigid Nonjuring orthodoxy, warned his flock of the dangers inherent in allowing themselves to be biased by such a view, and Grascome gave a categorical negative when asked whether attendance at a Parish Church was allowable to a Nonjuror. To him, non-communion was more forgivable than schism. It was, in fact, the general practice for Nonjurors to confine their acts of public worship to those occasions when they could meet with those of their own persuasion alone. The existence of these so-called

[1] *Of Christian Communion*, Part III, Chapter VII.

"Jacobite meetings" doubtless lent colour to a popular suspicion which regarded their members as politically dangerous, and helped to bring even some of the most peaceable into a disrepute which they would hardly have incurred had they been able to join in the ordinary service of the Revolution Church.

But apart from the question of the validity or otherwise of the ministrations of schismatics, the liturgy of the Revolution Church was a source of grave misgiving to the Nonjuring remnant. Although Archbishop Sancroft had composed and authorized for public use during the latter half of 1688 additional prayers which were so phrased as to be acceptable to either Jacobites or revolutionaries, once William had accepted the crown and created the schism, the deprived clergy were in nearly every case firm in their refusal to pray for the new King. Those parts of the liturgy which contained petitions for William and Mary in the stead of James, were branded as "immoral prayers," and thenceforward the rejection of their use was regarded as a test of Nonjuring orthodoxy. Hickes openly asserted that of the two sins he would greatly prefer to be guilty of attending the Roman Catholic mass than of taking part in "Such Offices wherein prayers are solemnly put up to God that are contrary to his essential justice and righteousness as lying is to his essential truth,"[1] prayers, that is, against a rightful Prince and on behalf of an usurper.

[1] *Dr. Hickes' answer to a query sent . . . by a Sergeant-at-law concerning communicating with a Church which prays for an usurper*, reprinted in *The Constitution of the Catholic Church and the Nature and Consequence of Schism*, 1716.

Humbler members of the Church, agreeing with Kettlewell that of the two evils, to be cut off from receiving communion altogether was worse than to receive it at the hands of schismatics, attempted to arrive at a compromise by attending the Parish Church services, but making some form of public protest against the actual petitions for the King and Queen. To this attitude the rigid Nonjurors were strongly averse, for in their opinion it was as unlawful for true Churchmen to attend services where prayers for an usurper were offered, even though openly dissenting from them, as it was for them to use the prayers themselves.

A further reason for the refusal of the Nonjuring clergy to attend, as lay worshippers, the regular services of the Revolution Church, was that by so doing they apparently accepted the authority of the secular power to deprive them. Only the Church itself, as representing Christ on earth, could discharge them from the active exercise of their priestly office. This the Church had not done, therefore they were still under the obligation of continuing to perform their function and to minister to their fellows.

But it is not for their views on the liturgy, the schism, or the oaths as such that the Nonjurors merit a place in the mainstream of English political thought. These controversies were but the eddies and whirlpools on the surface of the waters. Beneath and through them ran the current of a political faith which has a permanent interest and value far greater than that of the events which at the period of the Revolution determined its direction and disturbed its course. Contemporary events decided the form or shape through which the expression should be made, but the thoughts expressed arose out of certain fundamental notions concerning man in society. The real contribution which Nonjurors made to the political philosophy of their country lay deep in these underlying convictions about the need for moral sanctions in the community, the inescapable responsibilities of citizens to the spiritual no less than to the secular power, and the relationship of the State to those other associations, whether religious or not, which put forward a claim to the subject's allegiance.

4. *Religion as a Power in the State.*

It is not easy at first sight to determine how far the Nonjurors' theories were religious tenets finding expression through the organizations of secular society, or political faiths touched by religious enthusiasms. When, for instance, Grascome wrote: " It is the interest as well as the duty of Governors to advance the true religion and endeavour that it be embraced and practised by all. For then all their lawful commands will be executed with readiness, and the subject will obey for conscience' sake, which will make the Government strong, the people easy, and both safe,"[1] it is difficult to recognize the priest under the habits of the political platform orator. Religion there appeared as a sedative to calm the turbulent populace, a patent medicine to cure the ills of the State.

[1] *Moderation in Fashion*, Preface.

Elsewhere, the priest emerged, and supposing a case where " a Government requires something to be done which is sinful and unlawful, with which if the clergy will not comply, they shall be discharged from the exercise of their function and duty,"[1] found that in such a case God forbids compliance, and God must be obeyed rather than Government, even at the cost of imperilling the lives of his faithful people, otherwise the Cross would be denied and Christianity would be thrust out of the world. There a personal devotion to religion was ranked far above any thought of political expediency, and no thought of religion conceived as a means to the achievement of desired ends was allowed to outweigh the conception of it as the supreme good in itself.

This latter view is the truer expression of the Nonjuring attitude of mind towards the relation of religion to politics. Religion is not to be the servant of political ends except on its own terms. Nor for that matter need politics necessarily serve religion; but when it is within the power of either to serve the other, such service should be willingly given so long as it is possible without compromising the essential independence of each. The utilitarian view of religion as a vaccine to be injected under the patronage of a wordly-wise government which relies on piety as an inoculation against sedition, was one which entered only occasionally, and, as if by the accident of their psychological environment, into the arguments of the Nonjurors.

When they were able, as not infrequently they

[1] Grascome, *Reply to a Vindication of a Discourse.*

were, to escape from the confines of a philosophy which conceived of man as necessarily an irresponsible and licentious rebel, grounded his acts on a corrupt and evil human nature, and demanded that religion should be his taskmaster to keep him in order, they found their happier mental environment in those wide spaces of thought wherein he is seen as a creature, the very essence of whose nature it is to be religious, one who is internally bound by the spiritual chains of conscience to be the subject of a theocratic kingdom and the son of a divine Father. Nor is it as paradoxical as it appears to find these apparently contradictory views current among one body of thinkers, or even held by one man at different times. The history of plots and treasonable rebellion throughout the century was vivid enough to have given colour to the first, while the parallel history of the steadfast endurance of the High Anglican Church through all its vicissitudes left no room in their minds for doubt of the second. The one, though commonly connected with Calvinism, lent itself to an easy transmutation, and from being the sign of an extreme Puritanism it could be applied as an argument against those who had dealt so severely with the High Church Party, while the other had naturally developed into the Catholic doctrine of the independence of spiritual authority from secular control.

But to the vast majority of seventeenth-century minds in England religion was a synonym for Christianity, and to the members of the Anglican Church Christianity was supremely incorporated in and expressed through their own communion. Hence the abstract notion of an association between religion and politics became for them the concrete problem of the status of the Established Church.

Those moments, in which the idea of religion as an externally imposed obligation was paramount, were the times when the temptation to let the State use the Church was strongest, and the danger of falling into Erastian ways of thought greatest. When the Catholic temper prevailed, Erastianism was deemed accursed, and the idea of the independence of the Church as a spiritual body was of transcendent value.

But the tradition of the Establishment tended to produce a disharmony in the thought of the English Church, for the Nonjurors saw the possibility of Disestablishment towards which an uncurbed Catholicism might lead, while being unable to escape from the fact that the Established Church as they knew it had for over a century been the great bulwark against both Papists and Dissenters, both of whom they regarded as the enemies, not only of true religion, but also of the English Constitution. The problem for them was to discover the means by which these enemies of Church and State could be overcome without sacrificing the essential independence of the Catholic Church, and in the last resort, if no solution could be found, to witness to the supremacy of religious over secular allegiance.

The fact that all along their Church had preached the doctrine of the Divine Right of Kings and inculcated principles of unquestioning political loyalty in its members, made the decision infinitely harder. The measure of its hardness is the test of the sincerity of those whose loyalty to the Catholic ideal persisted even though it brought them into disrepute with their fellow-citizens for seeming lack of regard for the safety of the State, no less than with their fellow-Churchmen for their elevation of a difficult truth above a cherished unity. With the plea that the Christian religion is the greatest security of government, because it requires obedience and suffering, the Nonjurors could heartily agree. What they denied was that a religion whose priests allowed themselves to be controlled, in respect to their priestly function, by a secular power, continued to be Christian, and that the obedience and suffering required by Christianity were due on behalf of the State rather than of the Church itself.

5. *Inalienability of Spiritual Power.*

The Catholic conviction regarding the inalienability of the spiritual power was, as has already been said, the foundation upon which the Nonjuring Church was built. In the words of Hickes : " For Christian secular princes to drive rightful canonical bishops out of their thrones by secular force is plainly a dethroning or deposing of the spiritual sovereign by the spiritual subjects . . . and by consequence utter rebellion against Christ . . . as well as a violation of all order and an outrage upon the rights of the Church."[1] Not only so, but such an act was in the

[1] *On the Constitution of the Catholic Church*, Proposition 36.

nature of the case null and void, for the spiritual power of bishops was a grant from Christ and there could be no remission of its exercise except by his authority. Hence, though bishops might be fined, imprisoned, excluded from the enjoyment of their temporal estates, or otherwise punished, even to the point of death, they could not abandon their spiritual office at the behest of a secular power. Such submission would involve giving the State authority over Christ himself, which was unthinkable. The priest is for ever answerable for the use of his spiritual power, to him who originally granted it.

That there were political implications of this doctrine potentially dangerous to a state based on the absolute sovereignty of the secular Prince, is undeniable. For a Prince whose goal was absolutism to allow the claim of any of his subjects to owe allegiance to any other lord, was to open the door to another claimant for his authority in any sphere. Even when absolutism had ostensibly given place to a limited monarchy, the monarch's claim to sovereignty left no room for possible rivals. The English Constitution had achieved this independence for its sovereign only after a great struggle against the Papacy on the one hand, and the popular power on the other. The strong terms of the Oath of Supremacy witnessed to the depth of feeling against outside interference which accompanied the passionate assertion of this independence, and if the allegiance of the Church to the Pope was so wholeheartedly condemned, it was no less risky for the Crown to allow the clergy's claim to pay allegiance directly to the overlordship of Christ. The royal titles of Defender of the Faith and Governor of the Church, and the terms of the Establishment were all means by which an effort was made to concentrate power in secular hands at the expense of sacred. But the chief attempt to obviate the risks attendant upon the acknowledgment of a supreme authority apart from the Crown, had been expressed in the doctrine of the Divine Right of Kings. The King had been regarded as God's vicegerent, and therefore, in paying obedience to him, his subjects were to consider that they paid it to his and their Lord in Heaven. Thus their desire to obey God rather than man, was converted into a belief that they could obey God through man, by obeying the commands of his deputy, the King. No one was more devoted to this conception of obedience than were the Nonjurors, and it was in order to make it compatible with their principles concerning the inalienability of spiritual power, and the direct duty of the priesthood to God that they elaborated their theory of Church–State relationships.

6. *The Church as a Spiritual Society.*

"We are members of two great Societies," wrote Kettlewell, in one of his most popular books.[1] "One a society in things outward and temporal, for our happiness in this world, which is called the State; and the other in things sacred, spiritual and eternal,

---

[1] *The Measures of Christian Obedience*, 1681, which reached a sixth edition in 1714.

for our happiness in the next world, which is the Church ; and God has His representatives or vicegerents in them both." These both are, in a sense, divine, acknowledging the same Head. Rebellion in the one and schism in the other are equally damnable. Both are subject to the same kind of government—monarchical, for as the King and his ministers are to the State, so are the Bishops and clergy to their dioceses. Popular government is fatal to both, for it supposes the people, as possessors of the ultimate authority, to be above God. But membership in the first society is involuntary, and precedes membership of the second in point of time. Yet, on the other hand, the final allegiance of the subject belongs to the spiritual and not to the secular society. " It is happy for that nation where true religion is established by law," wrote Grascome, " but the truth and validity of it is antecedent to any such legal establishment, and it hath not its authority from the civil sanction, though it is more comfortably exercised under its protection. But if the civil power not only will not protect, but doth persecute the true religion, we must not renounce it unless we will forfeit our title to Heaven."[1] In what then does the real relationship between Church and State consist ?

Kettlewell's discussion of this relationship in his book, *Of Christian Communion to be Kept in the Unity of Christ's Church*, was the most coherent account of the Nonjuring view on this point apart from Leslie's *Case of the Regale. Of Christian Communion* emphasizes the reciprocal nature of the bond which ties

[1] *Moderation in Fashion*, p. 131.

Church and State. "In Christian Kingdoms the Church is incorporated into the State, and by the benefit of this incorporation Bishops and Pastors have their spiritual ministrations backed with secular effects and censures [*e.g.*, excommunication incapacities from civil and temporal privileges]. All these secular fortifications, jurisdictions and encouragements in their ministrations, conferred on Bishops and Pastors of an incorporate Church, are the gifts of the State and are secular additions to what spiritual powers they received from Jesus Christ. And what the State gives, the State when it sees cause may deprive them of."[1]

But the Church, in gratitude for these benefits and temporal accessions, has by compromise given up some of her own privileges to the secular power, notably the nomination of Bishops and Metropolitans, the right of her synods to regard their rules as canons prior to the approval and ratification by the Prince, and their right to refuse cures to clerks or to impose discipline except with the co-operation and consent of the laws of the land. The clergy are all subjects of the civil State, and can claim no exemption from the jurisdiction of its courts in civil or criminal cases, and "although the State has no power either to give or to deprive the ministers of Christ of their mere spiritual powers, yet it has a direct authority to grant and deprive them of their temporal additions."[2] Hence, if deprived, not by any ecclesiastical court on account of crime or heresy, but

---

[1] Kettlewell, *Of Christian Communion*, Part II, Chapter I.
[2] *Ibid.*

only by the State, while the clergy have no right to claim the appropriation of tithes or the use of the Parish Church buildings, they have no option but to continue their spiritual ministry. Similarly, the synods of the Church are also in a position of submission to the State in that they cannot pass measures, obliging Churchmen to disobey it, nor refuse to assemble at the State's behest, and that all their measures are subject to civil corroboration; but they may, if they see fit, assemble themselves to transact the business of the Church without waiting for the Prince's summons.

The position of the King himself in the Church is that of a subject. As Hickes pointed out, he, no less than other men, becomes subject to the Church by baptism, and the only difference between his position and that of any other member is on the debit side; he gets no more from the Church, but is under an even greater obligation than other men to defend her rights. But the rulers of the Church lose no shred of their authority by admitting a temporal ruler into membership. In spiritual affairs they rule a Prince as any other man, and may impose discipline upon him even to the point of excommunication. In temporal affairs the membership of a sovereign Prince in the Church in his domain is followed by " the coalescence or union of the Church with the State,"[1] but this " union or interweaving of the civil with the ecclesiastical laws of government . . . gives the State no more right or pretence of right to usurp it over the Church or invade its

[1] Hickes, *Constitution of the Catholic Church*, Proposition 20.

spiritual rights, which it derives from Christ, than it gives the Church to usurp it over the State, or invade its temporal rights which it derives from God."[1]

Any attempt by the State, therefore, to prevent rightful Bishops and clergy from performing their spiritual functions, or their flocks from participating therein, would constitute such an usurpation and dissolve the union; as also would persecution of the Church for her profession of any article of Christian faith. The dissolution would naturally involve the withdrawal of State protection of the Church. If either Church or State invades the rights of the other, then faithful subjects of the wronged party are bound to undergo all hazards and persecutions in defence of the threatened rights. But the concessions on each side being granted only on condition that their use should not in any way be prejudical to either, once the union is broken the recessions made by the Church to the State become void. All original powers which were granted to her by Christ and pre-existed the act of incorporation are regained.

It has always been the plea of Catholic Churchmen, that in holding to the truth as they see it, they are maintaining the traditions of the primitive Church, and that only so is it possible to discover purity of doctrine. Innovation in religion is to them fraught with the greatest possible danger. Impatient Protestants may accuse them paradoxically of making their ideal of progress retrogressive, of looking backwards in time and forward beyond time to find

[1] Hickes, *Constitution of the Catholic Church*, Proposition 24.

their standard of perfection, but never of expecting the Kingdom of Heaven to come on earth through the labours of Christians in the world here and now. The Nonjurors were as true to type as their Protestant contemporaries. They could not compromise with the Revolution Church, for to do so would belie their Catholic faith. The alliance of the Church with the State was indeed " happy " and " comfortable " so long as it did not demand the denial of the Catholic principle of the absolute spiritual automony of the Church. Once that principle was jeopardized by the new King the essential paramountcy of truth over unity obliged the High Church Party to refuse their participation in the new union which William desired to make with the Anglican Church, even though the old was but precariously cemented between a Popish Prince and a non-Roman Communion.

The civil rights of the subject were in every case the concessions of grace granted by the sovereign, who could recover them at will, leaving the subject scarcely more than a slave. The ecclesiastical rights of the Church, or the temporal additions pertaining to the Establishment, were similarly grants made by royal favour, equally recoverable, and liable equally to place members of the Established Church in the position of persecuted outcasts. But the spiritual rights of Christians were inherent in Christians as men, not as subjects or as belonging to the Establishment. These no civil sovereign could ever touch, and no Christian could ever forfeit to a civil power.

It was upon these rights that King William had

endeavoured to encroach when, through the secular acts of his so-called Parliament, he had ordered the suspension and subsequent deprivation of the Fathers of the Church. To allow for one moment that he was within his province so to do, would be to allow the secular power to usurp the authority of the spiritual, to " make it impossible for the Catholic Church to subsist as distinct and independent from the State, which will fundamentally overthrow the very being of the Church as a Society."[1]

[1] Kettlewell, *Letter to Dr. Tillotson*, May, 1691.

CHAPTER VI

CHARLES LESLIE

1. *Controversialist and Nonjuror.*

CHARLES LESLIE, though of Scottish descent and Irish up-bringing, has always been counted, and rightly so, as belonging to the English group of Nonjurors. His legal training, to which doubtless he owed no little of his ability and persuasiveness in controversy, was taken in England, and it was to London that he retired on being deprived of the Chancellorship of Connor for refusing the oaths in 1689. Thereafter, with the exception of one visit to his Irish estate in 1691, he returned there only to die thirty years later. The intervening years were passed chiefly in England, with periods of residence at the court of the exiled Stuarts. For a time he held a chaplaincy in the household of the Earl of Clarendon, and he was an occasional minister to Nonjuring congregations in London, but in spite of the fact that he was an intimate friend of Henry Dodwell, and well known to the Shottesbrooke group and other prominent Nonjurors, he seems not to have taken as important a place in the councils of the Party as his ability and energy would warrant. This may be accounted for by the very vigour of his character, which led him more than once to overleap discretion, and by consequence made it necessary for his own safety that he should avoid the public eye.

His father, the centenarian Bishop of Clogher, had all his life been inspired by a royalism " of the most vivid hue,"[1] and Leslie himself was but carrying on the family tradition when he engaged in even the most picturesque of his adventures. The Bishop who, when nearly ninety years of age, had ridden from Chester to London in twenty-four hours in order to pay his homage to Charles II. at the time of the Restoration, would have rejoiced at the sight of his son living in hiding, and even disguised in regimentals, for the best part of a year in order to avoid arrest after joining issue with those redoubtable princes of the Revolution Church, Bishops Burnet and Hoadly.

Leslie was without doubt the most brilliant of the Nonjurors, the most untiring of Conservative iconoclasts. Whigs, Agnostics, Deists, Jews, Quakers, Dissenters of every shade, even Churchmen of every party but his own—all were the object of his attacks. To the force of his reasoning there was added a power of ridicule, touched sometimes with a ringing sarcasm and at others with a genial humour. The combination made him a formidable opponent indeed.

But notwithstanding his controversial temper, it yet remained true that he regarded those with whom he disagreed not so much as his personal enemies, but as the adversaries of the God whose ardent servant he was. His partisanship did not cut him

[1] *Dictionary of National Biography*, XI, 980.

off from personal friendship with those whose convictions differed materially from his own, but neither could his friendship obviate the imperative necessity which he felt of giving expression to the principles by which he lived.

2. *Theory of State Sovereignty.*

The supreme fact of Leslie's political philosophy had its foundations in his certainty of the divine over-ruling of the universe. "Whatever founds government," he wrote, "must be superior to it, and above it. Government must derive its original and whole authority from it, and must be accountable to it, and dissolvable by it at its pleasure whenever it thinks fit. Now human cannot be superior to human. Therefore, Government among men cannot be derived from mere human authority. This is so very obvious that all Governments whatever, of whatsoever sort, and among all nations and religions, do pretend to a Divine Right."[1] Government might indeed be regarded by the impatient as " yoke under which God has placed us for our good,"[2] but the bearing of that yoke was, in Leslie's view, the price of safety for man, a safety which could never be contrived out of any merely human institution. " Government in the very nature of the thing does suppose an authority more than human," he wrote again, " for the same power that can oblige may likewise dissolve that obligation. So that men

[1] *Rehearsal*, I, 53.
[2] *The New Association*, Part I, Supplement.

might ever free themselves from government if it had no higher authority than that of man. Nothing under God can bind the conscience."[1] And this " authority more than human " was the source of all power, authority and right on earth. " If there is no Divine Right, there is no human right . . . For that all Right is derivative but God's. We must hold of some or other till we come to the first giver which is God . . . All Right is Divine Right and there can be none other, because God is the only fountain of all Right and Authority."[2]

But God delegates his power to earthly rulers, who mediate it in their turn to lesser magistrates. Thus, though all civil authority is ultimately from God, it is granted directly to no one but the supreme powers on earth, and all subordinate magistrates can receive it only through them. " There is or can be no civil authority in the Kingdom but what is derived from the Crown as the only fountain and source of all human authority. There can be no co-ordinate powers in the same government, nor balancing of power. It is all nonsense and contradiction. It is civil war instead of government."[3] The conception of the unitary nature of power was fundamental to all Leslie's political theory. The phrase, " all power is one and indivisible," recurs in his writings as a refrain. He flatly denied that in the last analysis any other kind of government but monarchy was anywhere discoverable. The species of government he saw was determined by three tests. The last resort or final arbiter in all disputes was

[1] *Rehearsal*, III, 13.   [2] *Ibid*, IV, 46.   [3] *Ibid*, III, 28.

the supreme governor, and without a last resort there could be no government. The ultimate source, under God, of civil authority was the supreme ; the one, that is to say, who granted all commissions to the subordinate rulers, but himself had no commission from anyone in the government. Thirdly, he who, being himself free from all coercion and punishment, while having the power to coerce or punish others, was again the supreme. But that any other authority short of a single monarch should incorporate in itself these three attributes was to Leslie incredible. The supremacy in every case must ultimately lie in one, either a body of people or a person, but even if it is supposed to lie in a body or assembly, any act or decision made by it " is not considered by the plurality of the persons, but by the unity of the body. And he that hath the casting vote is, in that, absolute and arbitrary. So that every government ends in a monarchy still, whatever schemes and devices we can find out to avoid it . . . the supremacy is indivisible. And both the legislative and the executive are in it. They are not two powers, but a different exercise of the same power— one to make a law, the other to see it executed. And the executive must judge of the law. So they are both the same . . . both are derived from the same fountain. For as no man can execute a law but by commission from the King, so no man has any vote in the framing of a law but wholly and solely from the King."[1]

In the English Constitution, as Leslie saw it, the

[1] *Rehearsal*, III, 22.

King is in fact himself the legislative power. He maintains the law, but does not submit to it. The Lords advise, the Commons petition, but the King alone enacts. The law itself is a dead letter until pronounced by a living authority, and once it is pronounced no exceptions can ever be permitted other than those which may be explicit in its formulation. "Surely we cannot except where the law does not except, else every man might except himself," wrote Leslie to Bishop Hoadly. "A reserve is nothing else but an exception of such a case or person. Whoever has power to make reserves in laws has the whole legislature in his own hands. A reserve is nothing where there is not coercion to enforce it . . . what signifies a law when there is no authority to put it into execution? But the law allows of no authority superior to the King, and bars all coercion upon him, therefore the law bars all reserves."[1]

Not only is the King the legislative and executive authority but the third great governmental function is equally his. He is the judicial authority. "The decision of all civil cases whatsoever," wrote Leslie, "is only by Authority. It is not law, justice or reason ever yet decided any such cause or ever can. These indeed are rules by which a judge ought to go. But if he does not, his decree stands good till reversed by a higher authority. So that authority is still the whole . . . It is not the King's will that [the judge] should do any injustice, and when he does so he goes against the King's will, but still acts by the

[1] *Finishing Stroke.*

King's commission, and has his authority for what he does, which defends him from all violence in the execution of his office."[1] In the same way, a King who does evil does it by his own will, and not the will of God, but he cannot be deprived of his commission for so doing by anyone save God who granted it, " so to punish Kings and take their commission from them is no less than aspiring to be God and to take the government out of his hands."[2]

That supreme power should be divided between a number of individuals was, to Leslie, sheer impossibility. "Does not all the world confess it," he asked, "that the collective body of the people cannot govern itself more than every man in the nation can be king? Well, then, will they let the body represented (according to their own schemes) be the *dernier ressort?* and must we take their voice as the voice of God? The senselessness of such schemes is nauseous. But if it was not destructive, too, we could bear it better. . . . All power is one and indivisible, whether in the hands of one or many. And several independent powers in the same government is anarchy and confusion. And is set up by none but who are laying seed-plots for Rebellion or who are besotted in their understanding."[3]

Leslie's theory of the origins of government[4] was a further demonstration of his conviction that supremacy must always reside in one individual. On this view the supreme power could not be in an

---

[1] *Best Answer Ever was Made.* [2] *Ibid.*
[3] *New Association*, Part II, Supplement.
[4] See Chapter II, pp. 71–75.

assembly because, although Parliament may be a part of the State Constitution, "it is an human constitution ordained of man. The Crown is a Constitution. But it is divine. That is ordained of God. And it is prior to that of Parliaments."[1] " If God had ordained Parliament at the same time with Kings and independent upon them they had been co-ordinated powers. But this our law abhors and makes it a traitorous position . . . And makes the Parliament the King's most obedient and dutiful subjects and not his peers."[2]

That which, according to Scripture, is expressly ordained of God, must be not merely the best but the only form of government approved among people who profess any belief in a Theocratic universe. As Leslie pointed out, to say that the authority of Kings or priests was derived from God, and then to declare that they were subject to control or coercion by the people, was no less than blasphemous, because it was tantamount to a declaration that God himself was subject, and a subject God would cease to be God at all.

Further, the supremacy, once having been granted by God, cannot be altered or given up by the Crown, for if it could it would be self-creative. Much less can it be invaded by the people. A limitation by coercion, even if self-imposed by the King, would, according to Leslie, involve the immediate dissolution of government. Coercion over the Crown is a contradiction of terms, leading as it does to a position in which the subjects assume supremacy and the

[1] *Rehearsal*, I, 140.   [2] *Ibid*, 139.

King becomes subject. He condemned even the suggestion of interference, however mild. "I do not think it proper," he declared, "for me or any private man to be thrusting in his oar in State affairs when he is not called upon for it . . . I know no liberty of the subject empowers him to this more than it is the right of every Englishman to be a Privy Councillor. And I think such a practice prejudicial to any Government."[1]

To Leslie it was impossible that a monarchical constitution should contain any errors; equally impossible that any other could permanently carry on government at all. The rulers would indeed never be safe against grievances and complaints, for miscarriages of justice were always liable to occur while the fallibility of men rendered mistakes of administration inevitable. "There will," he said, "be maladministration in every government while it is in the hands of men. And in every sort and species of government. For none are free from it. But an error in the Constitution is fatal, because it admits of no remedy, nor can be amended without altering the Constitution."[2]

But even were errors admitted to exist, the Constitution was, in Leslie's theory, of such rigidity that it was not open to alteration except on the dissolution of the body politic. A revolution does not destroy the government against which it is organized, but merely effects a change in the personnel of the administration. In a rebellion, the leaders persuade their followers that great benefits will accrue to them

[1] *Rehearsal*, I, 11.   [2] *Ibid*, III, 17.

in the result, but at the end a party wins and seizes power, and the people gain nothing. The administration may pass from one faction to another, but, however often it changes hands, government never dissolves altogether, nor does a change benefit the general body of the people. A faction has no mercy, and there is no legal remedy against it.

But if it were impossible for the Constitution to be fundamentally altered by rebellion or revolution, to alter it by the less violent method of legal processes was no less difficult, because it existed before all laws, and therefore could not be affected by the acts of legislators whose power was not coexistent in time with its own. In England the root and basis of the Constitution is the Crown free from all coercion. " The laws flow from our Constitution, therefore are not it, and the Constitution which makes our laws must be prior to those laws, and cannot be made by them."[1] Legislators are bound by the acts of their predecessors to keep laws which affect the Constitution, such as those touching on hereditary succession, but " their predecessors did not bind them from repealing any laws made by them. For they knew that the same authority which enacts can annul."[2]

Short of the occurrence of that one dire catastrophe which should cause the complete disruption of the body politic, the Constitution was immune from change, but at "that moment that coercion is granted over the king the government is dissolved and he is king no more. And all the authority in

[1] *Rehearsal*, I, 136. [2] *Ibid*.

the Kingdom flowing from the Crown, as has been said, consequently all is dissolved and our constitution is broken."[1]

Leslie, in this argument, apparently confessed that the English Constitution had suffered dissolution in 1648, but that the Revolution of 1688 was, in contrast, merely a change in the personnel of government, for there had been no counterpart of the regicide policy in the dealings of either the English people or the Prince of Orange with James II. In fact, this would only be true if the word "coercion" had no implications other than physical, but for Leslie the assumption of sovereignty by the body of the people was equally a coercive act. It was natural enough for a man of his strong political and ecclesiastical opinions to see "disruption" written large over his country's history in the middle of the seventeenth century. It would have been strange had he not seen it as plainly on the pages dated 1688-9. The fact that James II. happened to lack the courage displayed by his father, and that thus he escaped the ignominy of being physically coerced by his subjects through the simple expedient of running away, did not really make any fundamental difference to the nature of the two Revolutions. In both cases the disappearance of the King was an effect, not a cause, of the Revolution. In both cases the real Revolution was the assumption of sovereignty by the people of the realm, and the exercise of the assumed authority in disregard of the theory that sovereignty was inherent only in the person of the King.

[1] *Rehearsal*, I, 136.

Commonwealths and elective governments were, to Leslie, " preternatural and eccentric " or " bastard governments," but just as it is wrong to murder a bastard because, in spite of all, he is a man, so it is equally wrong to disobey these ill-begotten governments because they are governments and " none has a right to dispossess them but who have a better right to the government than they have."[1] Nor did this attitude towards a revolutionary government involve him in offering a justification of such ; it was but another illustration of his firm adherence to the principle of moral right underlying all government. Had he been sure of success in any serious attempt to restore the direct Stuart line to the throne, he probably would have become an active Jacobite plotter, but he respected moral order and abhorred force far too much to allow himself to be entangled in any movement against a settled administration unless he was certain that the issue would be favourable to his cause.

Most of Leslie's political works were written at a period some years subsequent to the Revolution; his theories, therefore, were inevitably modified by the circumstances of his time. The episodes of the Revolution, incidents such as Sherlock's compliance for example, which had roused Kettlewell and others to such a white-hot ardour, had necessarily directed the emphasis of their arguments towards the particular details of the political crisis through which they were living. After ten years Leslie was able to some extent to escape the particular, and devote his

[1] *Rehearsal*, I, 250.

mind to the more general aspect of political theory. He had observed the operations of the government of William and Mary and, while deploring its origin, he could not but acknowledge that it was fulfilling its function. The fundamental allegiance of Leslie's mind was to monarchical government in the abstract. The accidental circumstances surrounding the accession of William and Mary had forced him into opposition to their rule, and his views on hereditary succession kept him there immovably, but his devotion to the cause of Divine Right was of such a quality that he could, if necessary, disregard a lack of good title to the throne sooner than give up his defence of the throne itself. Writing in the first decade of the eighteenth century, he was not so much the defender of James II against the Revolution settlement, as the champion of a unitary sovereign power against the Whig theory of popular government. Hence he was able actually to carry over his doctrine of non-resistance into an advocacy of obedience in civil affairs to the post-Revolution government on the grounds that the government of any King was better for the nation than government by a mob, which was no government at all. And as long as the rightful King could not, or would not, exercise his authority, the people were wiser to obey that authority which was obviously expressed through the government of him or her who was the actual possessor of the crown, even though the possession was not based on the right of direct hereditary succession.

Leslie did not shrink from the corollary of his

theory of Sovereignty. If it were true that all authority was God-given, the fact that the obedience of the subject was also the ordinance of God was no less true. He insisted again and again that the unitary Sovereign was arbitrary and despotic, and had absolute authority over the lives of all his subjects. "What is birthright?" he asked, and there was no ambiguity in his reply: "If being born under laws and a government whose legislature has an absolute and despotic and unaccountable power over our very lives as well as our estates without staying to ask our consent, if this is to be free-born, then all the world are so, and ever have been so since Adam. Otherwise not one, unless a king be born after his father is dead."[1]

The arbitrary character of government was to Leslie its most essential feature. The supreme authority in any nation was he who was accountable to none but God, and was therefore potentially a despot in his relations with his subjects, although, by a voluntary limitation, he might cloak his despotism in benevolence. But, tyrannical or benevolent as the Sovereign might be, in the result it made no difference to the obligation of the subject. "We must be subject to the government either absolutely or conditionally," wrote Leslie; "if conditionally, who is judge of the conditions? If every man is judge, then every man may take arms and overturn the government when he pleases. And there is no other choice but absolute subjection."[2] And again, "The legislative power, wherever it is

[1] *New Association*, Part I.   [2] *Rehearsal*, III, 7.

placed in any sort of government, is and must be arbitrary and absolute, and it is impossible to be otherwise. And every man sees it in all government upon the face of the earth. The legislature is not bound to its own laws, but may repeal them at pleasure. And before repeal may dispense with them; and leap over them, and act contrary to them . . . in short may do what they will and make what they will to be law. For their will is the law."[1]

But the authority of the legislative power was a commission from God; hence it followed in Leslie's theory "that there is no rebellion whatever but against God, for all order and government on Earth as well as in Heaven . . . being the positive institution of God, consequently all disobedience to government or rising up against it is a rebellion against God the institutor."[2] He was as ardent in upholding the doctrine of non-resistance as was any member of his Party. For the subject to resist the Sovereign was not only to rebel against God, but was the worst possible way to achieve that security of life and property which it was a function of the State to maintain. An attitude of dutiful submission on the part of the subject, coupled, wherever possible, with a loyal support of the throne, was the best guarantee against tyranny in the ruling powers.

In spite of his insistence on the arbitrary power of the Sovereign and the unconditional obedience of the subject, Leslie did admit that the English Constitution allowed room for the relaxation of these

[1] *Rehearsal*, I, 38. [2] *Ibid*, 54.

principles in practice, even if not in theory. The Sovereign, in the aloofness of his absolute authority, was not a Great Mogul unbounded by any law : " He is bound. ·And bound by all the ties that are possible to bind a king. He is bound by his oath to God at his coronation, as well as his promise to his people. He is bound by all the laws of justice and honour. And . . . by his interest, too. Which with some is the strongest tie, for it cannot be his interest to provoke his people, lest factions should arise. . .
Now these are all the ties possible to bind a king, except that of coercion. And that cannot be without a dissolution of the whole government. . . . The king has bound himself neither to make nor repeal our laws without consent of Parliament. And the forms and methods of trials are regulated by our laws."[1]

The subject, on the other hand, enjoys a semblance of rights in the liberties explicit in the laws, in the right to a fair trial, and, up to a point, in the right to own property. " We have a divine right to our liberty and property in so much that whoever invades these unjustly is guilty of a sin against God. Even our governors are answerable to God if they deprive us of these without just cause."[2] But none of these " rights " of the subject are absolute in the sense that those of the sovereign can be called absolute. " All authority in the subject, and right to his possession flows from the Crown and returns to it again as to its source and original."[3] Leslie stood in the direct line between Machiavelli and

[1] *Rehearsal*, I, 140.   [2] *Ibid*, 102.   [3] *Ibid*, IV, 46.

Austin, when he insisted on the omnicompetence of the State. Everything which the subject owned or did belonged to him or was done by him only through the favour of the sovereign. In this view so-called " rights " were in reality but privileges to be granted or withheld at the will of the supreme ruler. " What birthright, what freedom, what liberty or property has a man but what is given to him by the laws of the land, and by the same may be taken away ? "[1] asked Leslie, and his answer is to be found in his development of the concession theory.

In this theory, not only were the rights of the subject *qua* individual wholly dependent on the will of the sovereign, but a similar limitation of dependence governed the rights of subjects as members of associations within the State. A wise king would grant to his subjects all concessions compatible with his own sovereignty and the safety of the State, for contentment in the general body of citizens leads to a dutiful loyalty to the Crown ; but true wisdom would be equally concerned in ensuring that the enjoyment of no concession ever exceeded the limits of its original grant. Particular care is necessary in the case of associations, lest, having been granted authority to meet and transact business relevant to the purpose for which they were formed, whether that purpose were religious, social, or any other, they should develop into a faction on a political basis, and become a danger to the State. But if authorised associations need careful watching, those which are formed without the permission of the

[1] *New Association*, Part I.

Sovereign are altogether anathema. " For subjects of their own heads, without the supreme authority, to enter into engagements, covenants and associations, has in all well-ordered States been ever counted a rebellion and treasonable, since it does, *ipso facto*, dissolve the government and tie such engagers and covenanters to other terms and conditions than the law hath appointed, and consequently of which the law cannot judge. This sets them above the law and puts the legislative power wholly into their hands. For that power cannot be parted, and he or they who can make one law may make a thousand, nay, must make all our laws and may repeal them all."[1] This particular attack was launched against the Scottish Presbyterian Church, and its violent phraseology may be somewhat discounted as the expression of a natural antipathy, felt by an ardent episcopalian for a sect whose form of Church government differed so radically from that which claimed his own allegiance, but the underlying meaning cannot be explained away. Leslie clearly denied any freedom of association to all subjects apart from the direct grant of the Crown.

Parallel with this strictly limited donation of rights, however, there was one sphere in which he conceded the absolute freedom of all human beings. A man's faith can be coerced by no one. Spiritually he is free. " God has subjected our lives and fortunes to the absolute disposal of civil government, because these are no great things, and we must give them up. . . . But God has taken more care of our souls,

[1] *New Association*, Part I, Supplement.

and not put our faith under the absolute dominion of any."[1]

Leslie saw where this would lead him and faced the consequences: "All the religions and all the sects in the world," he wrote in the same book, "are built upon the dispute between these two; whether men are to govern themselves by their own private judgment or to be determined by the authority of others in their faith and religion. Private judgment leads to multiplicity of sects and opinions, and hence to strife and war, both civil and national. But in spite of obvious disadvantages private judgment cannot be ruled out because ultimately it depends on private judgment what authority we select to be ruled by, and in the last resort, whether we believe in God at all."[2]

3. *The Sovereignty of the Church.*

Out of Leslie's attempt to reconcile the apparent discrepancy between his belief in absolute State Sovereignty and his faith in man's spiritual freedom arose his theory of the relationship between Church and State. The wide range of his vision and the depth of his insight enabled him to attain to an altogether bigger conception of the Church than that which found expression in the writings of the majority of his fellow Nonjurors. From his works there emerges an idea of the Catholic Church so vast and so profound that no claim which could be made on her behalf appears to demand too much, and no

[1] *Dissertation Concerning Private Judgment.*   [2] *Ibid.*

merely political organization could presume to dictate terms in its dealings with her. " The whole creation as well in Heaven as on Earth seems to be particularly designed with respect to the Church, and for her service and advantage,"[1] wrote Leslie, " God from the beginning of creation did erect his Church and preserved her as a visible and distinct society."[2] The head of the Church whence flows her authority is in Heaven, and as she was founded from the beginning independent of all powers on earth, so it is impossible that earthly powers should destroy her. This spiritual authority is supreme in its own sphere and is an essential quality of the Church's being ; no one can exercise it without being ordained thereto by God, and anyone hindering, or attempting to hinder, its exercise by those so ordained, is guilty of damnable sin.

But this great mystical society, the Catholic Church, was, in its earthly manifestation within the bounds of space and time, found to be a federal organization, the parts of which were separated, each under its own governor, and were as a rule localized and associated in some way with the several states of which their members were citizens. The universal and eternal Church, Catholic and Apostolic, was, in short, an association of a number of smaller Churches. " We do esteem every Bishop," wrote Leslie to the Bishop of Meaux, " with his college of Presbyters and Deacons and the Laity of his district, to be a particular Church, wherein the Bishop presides as representing the Person of Christ, and to be the

The Case of the Regale and the Pontificate, XX.   [2] *Ibid.*

Principle of Unity in his Church. . . . All particular Churches . . . make up the whole, which is the Catholic Church."[1] Elsewhere he declared that, " There were may be several societies independent of each other, *e.g.*, the Corporations in London, and Kingdoms in the Earth, yet all these may make up one Society . . . these are all different and independent societies with respect to each other, and have different rules and laws for governing their several bodies; but still with respect to the great body of which they are all members. Thus there are several societies in one society. And thus it is that the Church is a society in the great society of the world, and in the several Kingdoms and countries of it,"[2] but it is nevertheless one in its acknowledgment of the ultimate rule of the one God.

It appeared to Leslie necessary that any State professing a religion should have a Church established in its territory, for a Church was essential for the preservation of religion. By " establishment," he understood, " a Society under government professing some religion . . . and established by the laws of the land in opposition to others."[3] He further laid it down that " The government in Church and State must be alike. Kings are Bishops of the State, and Bishops are Kings and Princes of the Church."[4] " Both are the same species of government, that is, Monarchy, the one in the Church, the other in the State. And it is utterly inconsistent where the

---

[1] *The True Notion of a Catholic Church.*
[2] The second Part of *The Wolf Stripped.*
[3] *Rehearsal*, I, 27.   [4] *Ibid.*, II, 27.

Church and the State are incorporated to be for the one sort of government in the one, and the opposite sort in the other."[1] In this connection he recalled the famous dictum of James I.: "No Bishop, no King." The fortunes of the Church to which he himself belonged had during the preceding century fluctuated in a fashion illustrative of this maxim, and the period which saw the eclipse of both episcopacy and monarchy had seen the triumph of the Presbyterian Church. It was small wonder that the continued existence of the Episcopal Church as an independent society was inseparably connected in the minds of the Nonjurors with the perpetuation of monarchical government undiluted by popular control. The two ideas were interdependent, infidelity to the Church bred sedition in the State; rebellion in the State led to unfaithfulness in the Church. "Who allow no divine right in the Church can never find it in the State," wrote Leslie, "and whoever set up the power of the people must extend it to the Church as well as to the State. These go hand in hand together, for they set up the people in the place of God."[2]

In his discussion on the relationship existing between Church and State, Leslie was, of course, particularly concerned to discover the position of that unit of the whole Catholic Church which was established in England. It was distinguished from the Roman communion on the one hand by its rejection of Papal supremacy, and from the dissenters

[1] *New Association*, Part I, Supplement.
[2] *Rehearsal*, I, 248.

on the other by its insistence on the apostolic succession of the episcopate. In matters of doctrine subscription to the Apostles' Creed was the one condition required of members of the Church of England, the " indifferent things " (as Leslie termed ritual, vestments, etc.) " were never made by the Church any terms of communion."[1] He described its authority as " competent but not infallible,"[2] and stated that " our liturgy is an Act of Parliament."[3] Even though " our Church doth lawfully assert her own spiritual power entire and inherent in the Church . . . she hath always exercised her power in all subordination to the rights of Princes, and constantly acknowledging that whatsoever power besides spiritual the Church or its rulers have, she receives the same from the favour of our Kings."[4] Again: " the English Protestant Bishops and regular clergy as becometh good Christians and good subjects . . . acknowledge them [the Kings of England] to have sovereign power over them as well as over other subjects in all matters ecclesiastical as well as temporal."[5] Clearly, in matters of detail and organization, the separate units of the great world-wide spiritual society lose something of the purity which would ideally belong to the bride of Christ ; such purity as is imagined in the abstract is apt to become sullied in the process of embodiment in the particular.

In some forms of Church-State relationships, as

[1] *Rehearsal*, I, 20.
[2] *Dissertation Concerning Private Judgment.*
[3] *Case of the Regale*, XV.
[4] The second Part of *The Wolf Stripped.*   [5] *Ibid*.

Leslie pointed out, the two powers have frequently overstepped the boundaries of their own provinces, and gross abuse has resulted. "This exorbitant and wicked pretence set up by the Pope and the Presbyterians of extending the powers of the Church to a civil power, even to the deposing of Kings (as has been practised by them both) has rendered the true and only inherent *spiritual* power of the Church (which is independent of all earthly powers whatsoever) suspected to Kings and States, and given them occasion to exceed as much on the other side and lay their hands even upon the spiritual power of the Church, to curb, limit and garble it till they have squeezed the very life and soul out of it. Which is of no less evil consequence, not only to the souls of men and the efficacy of religion, but . . . to the civil government itself, by loosening the greatest security they have, which is the conscience of the people."[1]

But it was Leslie's claim for the Anglican Church that it was free from the dangers inherent in either the Papal or the Presbyterian organization. The principles of the Establishment in England, as he saw them, enabled the Church to escape from the Scylla of Erastianism, while at the same time the State could avoid the Charybdis of Papal control. His famous *Case of the Regale and the Pontificate* was an exhaustive discussion of these alternatives. The whole purpose of the book was to condemn on the one hand the assumption by the State of power over the Church with reference to her purely spiritual

[1] *New Association*, Part II.

authority, and on the other, the claim of the Pope to interfere in temporal affairs even to the point of deposing Kings.

Leslie asserted that in its historical aspect, the Regale or Erastian practice of the State had arisen in England through a grant of power made by the Popes to the Kings in order to minimize the power of the Bishops and thus ultimately to enlarge that of the Papacy; hence it was liable in the long run to swing the balance over to the other extreme and give birth to the Pontificate or Papal supremacy. But even before this came to pass the existence of the Regale seemed likely to produce crises in the life of the Church sufficient to diminish her vitality and influence almost to vanishing point. If Kings claimed authority over the Church as an inherent right of the Crown, it must follow that an infidel, or any other non-Churchman who happened to be the rightful King, could also claim it, and how could an unbeliever be the "supreme governor" of the Church, which, in fact, the King of England was, according to the phraseology of the Oath of Supremacy? The possession of the Regale was fraught with grave danger, not only to the Church as a society, but to the character both of the King and the clergy, tempting the former to hypocrisy, and the latter to fall into a secular mind. If it is in force, the Church must be, *ipso facto*, a party to all Revolutions, and hence fall into sin. Again, supposing that the Regale, instead of being a right inherent in the right of the Crown, was acquired by contract in return for State protection of the Church (an unproven supposition at the best), the relation between the Church and State would be no whit better, for then the one would be completely in subjection to the other and lose even the semblance of her independence. " If the power of one society extend likewise to the making of laws for another society (as if the Church could make laws for the State in temporals, or the State make laws binding the Church relating to spirituals), then is that society entirely subject to the other."[1]

Beyond and behind all other dangers of the Regale, however, lay the greatest danger of all, namely, that the Church, by being forced to render up her spiritual power into secular hands, would become so dependent on the State that religion would be turned into mere statecraft, lacking in all reality and mocking the God whom to reveal was the be-all and end-all of its existence. " No King or State can believe any Religion that depends on their authority, because then they must know that the origin of it is not divine,"[2] wrote Leslie, and he detected the evil effects of this shattering of belief already at work in the English people. He declared that "the Erastian principle has had two visible effects in England; that it had turned the gentry Deists; and the common people Dissenters . . . the Dissenters one and all pretend to divine commission independent of all the powers upon the Earth; therefore, the people run to them and look upon the Church of England as a Parliamentary religion, and the Establishment of the State. And the Deists . . .

[1] *The Case of the Regale*, III. [2] *Ibid.*, XVI.

can never think that there is anything divine in that which they see stand or fall by their vote."[1]

The one possible way out of the impasse caused by the Regale was, in Leslie's view, that the Church should make good her claim to complete spiritual independence. " The Right to meet, to consult, to make rules or canons for the regulation of the Society is essential to every society, as such, and consequently to the Church as she is a Society,"[2] this right the Church must never renounce, for it is essential to her being. Nothing short of insistence upon her continued existence as a society separate and distinct from the State could preserve her from extinction. She must be as ready to renounce her claim to authority in civil affairs as she was valiant to deny the like claim to interference in spiritual matters made by the State. " Let in the State upon the circumstances of the Church, or the Church upon those of the State. They will soon draw the essentials with them. Therefore, in order to their good agreement, it is necessary that they be kept wholly independent and unlimitable by one another in their several spheres."[3] " The medium betwixt these is plain, and is the Truth, which is, to keep those powers, the sacred and the civil as they are in their own nature, distinct and independent of each other. They act in two spheres, and, therefore, can never interfere. But if either encroach upon the other there is confusion without end or remedy."[4] The powers of both are derived from God, but those

---
[1] *The Case of the Regale*, V. [3] *Ibid.*, Supplement.
[2] *Ibid.*, Preface. [4] *The New Association*, Part II.

of one have reference to the soul of man, and may in their exercise extend beyond the bounds of this world and are operative into eternity, while those of the other are exercised only in respect to man's material nature while he dwells on earth.

But to say that the Church is and must always be a society independent of the State is not to say that there can be no recognized connection between them. To Leslie, the genius of the Anglican Establishment lay in this very fact that, through it, if rightly interpreted, the Church was enabled to maintain her independent existence as a spiritual society, while at the same time she gave moral support to, and received material support from, the political State. The members of the Church were answerable to the State in all civil matters, even the Bishops and clergy were subject in this sense. The State, on the other hand, could be called upon by the Church to add civil penalties to her ecclesiastical censures, and even the civil governors, as they were members of the Church's flock, were subject to her discipline in that capacity as much as were any others. Kings and Bishops had the right to mutual loyalty, though not to mutual appointment or deprivation. Once her purely spiritual authority is acknowledged by the State, the Church has gained all she needs to maintain her own independent being. She must not demand more and she cannot demand less. "As our Church doth lawfully assert her own spiritual power entire and inherent in the Church, so she hath always exercised her Power in all subordination to the Right of Princes. And constantly acknowledging that whatsoever power besides spiritual the Church or its rulers have, she receives the same from the favour of our Kings."[1]

Hence Leslie's final verdict on the problem of the relationship of the Church and the State was the assertion of their dualistic nature. Though both derived their authority from one source and both were ultimately subject to the one divine ruler, they were on earth two distinct and separate societies. The union between them, where such existed, was accidental and federal, and never incorporating. "They can never clash more than two parallel lines can meet, for they act in different spheres."[2]

---

[1] The second Part of *The Wolf Stripped*.
[2] *Rehearsal*, II, 27.

CHAPTER VII

LATER DEVELOPMENTS OF ANGLO-CATHOLIC POLITICAL THEORY

1. *The Doctrine of Divine Right.*

THE doctrine of the Divine Right of Kings had arisen in Europe during the conflict between the Holy Roman Empire and the Papacy. In its origins it was essentially anti-clerical. It had symbolized that unity of control which was so necessary for the development of independent nationalism. It grew into the theory of State Sovereignty and gave rise to the later conception of the omnipotence of law. But the doctrine was not the monopoly of any one nation, and it was naturally modified by the differing local circumstances of the countries where its influence was felt. Hence, in England, the Establishment of a National Church separate from Rome and the vicissitudes which that Church had endured during the century and a half subsequent to the Reformation, determined the particular forms in which the development of the doctrine became enshrined. It was in the interest of the National Church to foster the Divine Right theory with every possible care, for not only did her origin in part derive from it, but, as far as could be seen, her continued existence depended on it.

The Church as the *via media* between the two extremes of the Papacy and Presbyterianism preached the divinity of Kings as the price of her protection from both; while the Kings afraid, both of foreign interference and of the popular demands for power within the realm, supported the Church with which they found themselves in such precise agreement. This alliance had emerged triumphantly from the period in the middle of the seventeenth century when both its partners had suffered eclipse. The Restoration in 1660 had been an ecclesiastical no less than a political event. The common suffering and the common triumph only served to strengthen the interdependence of the parties. It was not until the defection of one of them from the fundamental principle of anti-Papalism, upon which the alliance was built, that a catastrophe became inevitable.

Its inevitability arose from the fact that ever since the Church and the Crown had been mutually guaranteeing each other's stability, they had regarded the theory of Divine Right as something static—a God-given formula which would serve their purpose and maintain their security for ever. They had forgotten that doctrines, like nations, can rise and fall, that an idea which is a novelty for one generation becomes a commonplace for the next and may be discarded by a third after it has fulfilled its original function. High Churchmen, with their Catholic bias, resisted Protestant tendencies in both Church and State. They were out of sympathy with the great majority in the nation which, having used the theory of Divine Right as a means of establishing

162 ALLEGIANCE IN CHURCH AND STATE

State sovereignty free from clerical control, was moving towards the establishment of the sovereignty of the people free in practice, if not in theory, from royal control, and based upon the opposing theory of the contract. In their reaction from these developments they had fallen back on their old defence and become even more ardent upholders of the theory in its earlier form. They were wholly unprepared with any political philosophy which could withstand the double shock of finding the Anglican Establishment persecuted by a Romish King, and a powerful majority in the nation prepared to deny the principle of indefeasible hereditary right, and to take the responsibility of inviting an alien ruler to come and protect the country and the constitution. If the doctrine of the Divine Right of Kings had not already by 1688 been more than half dead the Revolution could have been prevented by the action of the Church alone. That the number of bishops and clergy who accepted the Revolution Settlement and took the oaths was as large as it proved to be was itself an indication that there was no vitality left in the theory as a political force.

2. *The Political Issue.*

On the issue of Jacobitism as opposed to the Revolution Settlement, the Nonjurors were defeated by common sense and by James II. While they were arguing over the philosophical niceties involved in their avowal of loyalty to a King who would not rule, the rest of the country was busy living out in actual experience the more practical doctrine that, whatever happens to the King the government must never die, but must continue to function if the nation is to continue to exist. It was the flight of the *de jure* not the invasion of the *de facto* King which was, if they could but have seen it, the initial cause of their defeat. Had there been anything in James which could have made him worthy of his subjects' loyalty, that loyalty would have been forthcoming from all but a very few. As it was, the minority which still personalized the conception of Divine Right, had to blind itself to the obvious defects of the individual in whom they believed that right to be embodied, while the majority for whom the phrase " Divine Right " had come to be associated with government in the abstract, rather than with any individual personification of it, was ready enough to metamorphose the figurehead and transfer its allegiance when James proved unworthy.

The imposition of the oaths by William in 1689 was a State necessity, and the omission of the word " rightful " made them as easy as they well could be if they were to mean anything at all. But it is possible to argue that deprivation was a needlessly heavy penalty for those clergy whose dread of perjury made them unable to take them, and the Government might well have dispensed with the Oath of Abjuration in 1701. It is noticeable that the more reasonable and moderate among those who attacked the Nonjurors' position frankly admitted their right to refuse. Wise and good men might easily be extremely perplexed to know what course to adopt.

"A man's conscience," wrote Stillingfleet, "is his practical judgment concerning moral actions; and there are so many circumstances which vary the nature of such moral actions as oaths, that I do not wonder to see men differ about them."[1] But he went on to argue that " if there be a law which makes a contract void on account of the public good, the adding of an oath to such a contract doth not make it valid. . . . There is a common good of human society which mankind have an obligation to antecedent to that obligation they are under to particular persons . . . and it is agreed on all hands that an antecedent and superior obligation doth void that which is subsequent and inferior when they contradict each other."[2] The Nonjurors, with their minds still in those times when the public good of the nation apparently depended wholly on its independence from foreign control, and such independence was symbolized in the person of its rightful king, were, of course, unable to admit that allegiance to that king could ever in any circumstances be an inferior obligation. Stillingfleet and those of his kind who sincerely desired the best for their nation had moved with the times and could not fail to see that the public good could never be achieved under the misgovernment of James. To them, God's establishment of law and order for the public good was more important than his witness in the oath, " we say the former oath is not in force, as it is repugnant to the

[1] *A Discourse Concerning the Unreasonableness of the New Separation.*
[2] *Ibid.*

public good, and so the second may be taken without any contradiction."[1] The political philosophy of the Revolution period was already beginning to assimilate utilitarian conceptions. The High Church Party, which, after the Restoration, had shown signs of emergence from mediæval ways of thought was, in the stress of circumstances, returning to its text-flinging, or at the most was measuring utilitarian doctrine by the standards of Jewish and early Christian history instead of allowing it to be their standard on its own merits.

Leslie insisted that "it would be an affront to human understanding to follow the arguments of 'heathen authors' in political affairs in preference to the adoption of doctrine laid down in the Scriptures."[2] But while he was a true representative of his Party in declaring his adherence to "clear and undoubted authority which the Scriptures only are,"[3] he was more alive than many to the dangers of attempting to prove a case from analogy only, and deprecated the method of argument which would employ isolated instances for the purpose of such proof without regard to their relevance to current controversy.

The majority of Nonjuring controversialists, by their conservative habit of mind, were prone to regard the Old Testament account of God's dealing with the Jews as the pattern and ideal of all political relationships. This habit of seeing in Scripture the

[1] *A Discourse Concerning the Unreasonableness of the New Separation.*
[2] *The New Association*, Part II, Supplement.
[3] *Letter Concerning the New Separation.*

only revelation of the divine will and using the Old Testament as a text book of political practice precluded them from holding any belief in the subsequent development of governmental institutions. In minds which believe reform to be always retrogressive there can be no room for an evolutionary conception of politics. Seventeenth-century political speculation still moved within the orbit of a positive theocracy, and the spirit which was to inspire historical and anthropological research, as it had already been the inspiration of the scientific revival, had not yet deflected theological reasoning far from its customary path. Thinkers of a later age look elsewhere than in the books of Genesis or Kings for complete evidence of the origins of society and government, and do not regard the theory of Sovereignty whereby authority is derived from the direct gift of God as necessarily the final word on the subject. The theories of government held by the Nonjurors were static, and they failed to realize that the final word is just that which never can be said in reference to human society, for so long as society lives it must move and change. "What a dreadful thing this democracy is,"[1] was the impatient exclamation of another English Catholic, nearly two hundred years later; and although it was impossible to forecast in 1689 the form which the "dreadful thing" would assume, after 1832 and 1867 it was not impossible to see, for those who looked forward as well as back, that English society and institutions, no less than English

[1] John Henry, Cardinal Newman, in a letter to R.W. Church, 1885. Quoted in Wilfrid Ward's *Life*, Vol. II, p. 513.

thought, which had all been for generations in a perpetual state of flux, were likely to undergo changes at least as great as they had endured in the past. It was the belief that a change is always for the worse, that so hampered the conservative philosophy. "So much safer are we in the hands of God than of men," wrote Leslie, "in that government which he has established for the good of the people than in all their own contrivances of electing and deposing their own Kings and framing new schemes of government to themselves."[1]

The members of the Nonjuring minority survive in history not as a political power, but solely because they cherished the one remaining live issue in the theory of Divine Right. Their political theories have been rejected by later generations with the same ignominy as they were themselves rejected by their contemporaries. The growth of knowledge and the march of events have defeated, or are in process of defeating, the patriarchal theory of origins, the notion of absolute and arbitrary authority, the doctrines of unquestioned non-resistance and the concession theory of rights, just as the Revolution and Whiggism of 1688 defeated Sancroft and his followers. But in challenging the assumption of the lay power to control ecclesiastical affairs and in their unflinching insistence on the spiritual autonomy of the Church, the Nonjurors were not the conservative defenders of a forsaken belief, but were pioneering in the attempt to save the Church from Erastianism. Not only so, they were unwittingly but none the

[1] *The New Association*, Part II, Supplement.

less surely asserting the rights of individuals and minorities against the omnicompetence of the Hobbesian State, for to admit man's essential freedom in spiritual matters was to open the door for his claim to freedom in other directions also. They were helping to win freedom of conscience for the individual no less than that freedom which is so vitally necessary to the existence of associations within the State. If, on the " State Point," time has proved them to have been on the losing side, on the " Church Point " it has no less certainly been in their favour, though the complete liberation of the spiritual society from secular control which is the logical outcome of their position has not even yet been secured.

3. *The Relationship of Church and State.*

If the adoption of the doctrine of Divine Right by the radical thinkers towards the end of the seventeenth century, and its transfer by them from the person of kings to the ordinances of a humanly-appointed government, was a development which the Nonjurors were not prepared to accept, they, for their part, were not only willing but anxious to bring about its reincarnation as an ecclesiastical dogma. The ascription of Divine Right to the Pope which had been the keynote of mediæval thought had, for the majority of Englishmen, been abandoned after the Reformation in favour of its application to Kings. It was henceforward in the philosophy of Anglo-Catholics to be the prerogative of the Church primarily, and of Kings only so long as they did not interfere with the Church's spiritual autonomy. Even the claims of man's conscience as the voice of God in the soul could not be allowed to supersede the authority of the Church over the individual, for, having once acknowledged the divine Sovereignty over his life, man must be prepared to accept the Church's interpretation of that Sovereignty. This view almost insensibly involved its adherents in the beginnings of a movement towards toleration, or at least an admission that opinions other than those current in the Church of England were in fact held by large numbers of people, and though the expression of them must be carefully limited, their existence must be taken into account. Persecution might be expedient as a secular policy, but it was beginning to be regarded as illogical from a religious standpoint. Dissent was the mark of a crank, and those who professed it must not be allowed to hold public office. It was to be strictly discouraged, but where it existed it might, so long as it did not involve acts of hostility to the constitution and government of the country, be endured.

The one attitude towards the Church which the High Church Party would not tolerate in any circumstances was that which acknowledged her as subservient to the secular authority. The controversies which raged around this question during the first few years of the eighteenth century gave ample opportunity for High Churchmen to explain their position. Their spokesmen were to be found both within and without the Nonjuring camp. Leslie and Law of the former group, both came to feel a concern for the general application of the principles of the Church's spiritual independence, greater than that which they felt for the particular and accidental issues which determined their own peculiar position as non-members of the Revolution Church. Their loyalty to High Church principles made them the natural allies of men of similar allegiance even when they differed from them on the question of the oaths. Among these the most prominent was Francis Atterbury, who was outstanding for the protest which he made against the Erastianism of Wake, Hoadly, and the majority of the bishops.

The problem of the status of Convocation was, for some years, the chief point at issue in the struggle between the High and Low Church factions. From the time of the Revolution to the year 1700, Convocation never transacted any business. Its meetings were limited to the sheer formalities of assembly and dispersal at the command of the King. It had no voice in the government of the Church. Between 1700 and 1706 it was allowed to meet for the transaction of business on several occasions, and again between 1710 and 1717, but it was mainly occupied during these sessions in carrying on an undignified and inconclusive dispute between the Upper House, largely composed of Liberal, or Latitudinarian elements, and the Lower, which was preponderatingly High Church. From November, 1717, it ceased to function as a business assembly until 1852. This total eclipse of the Church's governing body was a triumph for Erastianism, but

LATER DEVELOPMENTS

it was not achieved without a struggle, nor did the High Church defeat involve the complete extinction of High Church principles.

The controversy had been aroused by the publication in 1697 of an anonymous *Letter to a Convocation Man*,[1] which had insisted that the King's summoning Convocation and allowing it to reassume its former legal powers of debate was the only method of combating the current evils in the Church throughout the country. Wake, then a royal chaplain and the incumbent of a fashionable London Church, and later to be Primate of England, replied with *The Authority of Christian Princes Over Ecclesiastical Synods Asserted* . . . In this book he unhesitatingly deduced from a mass of historical illustrations the right of the Sovereign not only to nominate, convene, and disperse the Synods of the Church at his pleasure, but also to govern the proceedings in respect both to the matter and method of debate, and to ratify or reject the conclusions at his will. " Certain it is that they may not so deliberate as to come to any authoritative resolution upon any particular point ; or to frame any order, or Constitution of what kind soever it be, without the King's leave ; which is in effect to say that they may not debate, synodically, at all, without it."[2] The limits within which the rights of Convocation were thus hedged, reduced the Church to such a position of

---

[1] The authorship of this letter has been attributed variously to Sir Bartholomew Shower, Dr. Binckes, and Atterbury himself ; it is probable that the first and last-named of these were jointly responsible. *Cf.* Sykes' *Edmund Gibson*, p. 27.

[2] *The Authority of Christian Princes*, Chapter III, §8.

subservience to State control that it became in effect little more than a department of government—a specialized "Watch Committee" to guard against possible tendencies of anti-governmental thought or action among the population. Lay power, to which Church appointments were already subject, could hardly go further.

Before his elevation to the See of Rochester, Francis Atterbury was the leader of the Lower House in its demand for ecclesiastical independence. He, in his *Rights, Powers and Privileges of an English Convocation Stated and Vindicated*, and Leslie, in *The Case of the Regale*, were concerned to maintain the position that the existence of a self-governing representative assembly wherein questions of dogma, order, and policy might be freely debated, was essential to the life of the Church as an independent society. Unless the Church had this mark of independence, she would not only cease to be a true Church, and hence lose her spiritual authority over her members, but also to the extent of that loss she would cease to perform her real function towards the State.

In replying to Wake, Atterbury discussed the status of Convocation in particular, vehemently denying that it was limited in its powers of debate, though agreeing that it could not assemble or enact new canons without royal authority. Leslie, looking at the wider implications of the spiritual independence (or bondage) of the Church, argued that "as it is rebellion and usurpation in the Church to extend her commission to civil power, so is it the highest sacrilege and rebellion against Christ for the civil power to extend its commission into the spiritual kingdom, and usurp upon the sacred office. It is confounding Heaven and Earth."[1] "No King or State," he added, "can believe any religion that depends on their authority, because then they know that the original of it is not divine."[2] By admitting the Divine Right of the Church to rule her own affairs, the State has nothing to lose and everything to gain, for, according to the terms of the Establishment, the Anglican Church is the ally of the State in the effort to overthrow foreign domination as well as in the preservation of peace at home by the insistence on the practice of passive obedience. "The State has no security so great as the principles of the people when they are taught to obey for conscience' sake and to believe that rebellion is a damning sin."[3]

The emphasis which the Nonjurors had always laid on the sinfulness of rebellion was naturally an embarrassment to the bishops and other Whig clergy who had participated in or acceded to the Revolution. The partial denial of it was the original cause, as early as 1705, of the prominence of Hoadly in the controversies surrounding the relationship of Church and State. By 1709, he was the avowed champion in the Church of the Whig doctrine of the Revolution, and the political leader of the Low Church clergy. But the full extent of his latitudinarianism was not realized until he attacked the High Church position in *A Preservative against*

---
[1] *Case of the Regale*, Chapter IV.
[2] *Ibid.*, XXI.   [3] *Ibid.*, V.

the Principles and Practices of the Non-jurors, which was his reply to the posthumous publication of George Hickes' *Constitution of the Catholic Church* ... in 1716. The discussion of Hoadly's *Preservative* and of one of his sermons by the Lower House of Convocation was the proximate cause of its prorogation in the following year. But the silencing of that organ of High Church opinion was but one incident in the Bangorian[1] controversy which carried on the dispute between High and Low Church with even greater acrimony though on a somewhat broader basis than the Convocation issue alone. Hoadly denied that the visible Church on earth was either directly or mediately governed by Christ, a denial which, of course, involved the rejection of the doctrine of Apostolic succession, and indeed of the conception of the Church as a spiritual society. The exaltation of the lay authority in all spheres of thought and action, whether religious or secular, followed inevitably from the refusal to acknowledge any supernatural character in the Church.

William Law was the ablest of the High Churchmen who strove to uphold the authority of the Church against this attack. He maintained that to allow sincerity to be an adequate test of fitness for salvation, as Hoadly did, was to invite error and heresy to take possession of the Church. It was, in fact, to abandon the Church's claim to be the guardian of truth and the channel of grace. But Law's voice was as that of one crying in the wilderness. The Nonjuring Church, of which he was so dis-

[1] Hoadly had been elevated to the See of Bangor in 1715.

tinguished a member, lost the capacity, as a Church, to raise any effective protest against the ever advancing Erastianism of the age. It was inevitable that as the events which had given it birth lost their significance through the lapse of time, it should gradually weaken its hold on its adherents. Its history is one of disunity and ever diminishing power.

But the body of doctrine which formed the basis of its life was not, mercifully for the Church at large, the monopoly of this shrinking and ineffective communion. The same vivid conviction which had inspired the early Nonjurors, namely, the realization of the essential nature of the Church as a spiritual society with a life of its own independent from that of the State, animated the life and thought of a few Churchmen who became prominent in the Establishment during the eighteenth century. To these the saving of Protestantism in England was a matter of cardinal importance. Its paramountcy over all other considerations, even over the saving of the legitimist line of the royal house, forced them into the adoption of Whiggism as a political creed. Tory clergy and Tory politicians alike were Jacobites. Jacobitism was seen to be intimately linked with Roman Catholicism. To preserve the country from civil war and the Church from Popish domination it was necessary to maintain at all costs the Hanoverian succession. The cost included the forging of a close alliance between the Whig supporters of the Revolution Settlement and the hierarchy of the Established Church. This alliance was largely the work of Bishop Gibson; its most prominent apologist was

Bishop Warburton. But though the means they were forced to adopt in order to save the very existence of the Church seemed to lead directly into the grossest Erastianism, the end which they strove to accomplish was the end dear to all High Churchmen. They realized that to exert every influence in order to preserve the being of the Church would be of little use, if, after all, there was found to be no Church left to preserve. They chose to save the life of the Establishment by losing it.

This apparently suicidal policy was, in fact, the only way of escape open. "It seemed to be," wrote Gibson's biographer, "not only the deliverance of the spiritual society, bound hand and foot, into the power of Cæsar, but its prostitution also to serve the ends of a single political party. Yet this servitude was proposed, and so far as circumstances would permit, translated into action, not by the Erastian Hoadly, whose views on ecclesiastical authority were notoriously lax, but by a prelate whom the satirists pilloried as the spiritual descendent of Archbishop Laud, the most dangerous enemy of the civil Constitution since his execution,"[1] one who "was the apostle of the divine right of the hierarchy and of the independence of the spiritual society . . . implacable in his hostility to all preachers of false doctrine."[2]

Warburton accepted the alliance as a *fait accompli*, and was supremely anxious that nothing should intervene to break the compact upon which he

---
[1] Norman Sykes, *Edmund Gibson, Bishop of London*, p. 119.
[2] *Ibid.*, p. 182.

LATER DEVELOPMENTS

believed it to rest. His defence of it was occasioned by the discussion on the proposal to repeal the Test and Corporation Acts in 1736. In his view, the Church had renounced supremacy over its own affairs to the State in order to secure State protection of the Establishment in return. " The great primary and fundamental article of Alliance is this," he wrote, " that the Church should apply all its influence in the service of the State, and that the State shall support and protect the Church."[1] The admission of Dissenters to posts of administrative authority which would have been achieved by a repeal of these Acts, would have resulted in the dilution of Church principles in the supreme governing body of the Church, or, in other words, would have been a repudiation of the compact on the part of the State by a radical alteration in its Constitution. Such a repudiation would automatically dissolve the Establishment, and the Church would recover the supremacy which it had resigned.

Warburton insisted that the theory of the alliance which he propounded was not a deduction from the status enjoyed by the Anglican Church, but was purely an abstract conception " founded in Nature and the invariable reason of things." The truth or falsehood of the religion so established was, in this sense, an irrelevant consideration. Public utility in itself demanded the establishment of some religion in every State. Nevertheless, he found the Christian religion to be well suited to this scheme, especially that variety of it which found expression in the

[1] *The Alliance Between Church and State*, p. 68.

Church of which he was not only a member but a Bishop. The importance of his reasoning in his *Alliance* did not lie in the conclusions to which the peculiar political situation of his time led him, but rather in the abstract premises of his argument. His consideration of the nature of Church and State as distinct entities was an essentially High Church view; his conclusion regarding their alliance was the result of the latitudinarian Whiggism which circumstances had forced his party to adopt.

The keynote of Warburton's position was his emphasis on the inherent and lively independence of the two societies, secular and religious, prior to the formation of the alliance between them. The religious society to him " must needs be sovereign and independent of the civil . . . there being no such agreement between two societies essentially different, there can possibly be no dependence. For that civil and religious societies are essentially different is evident from their having different ends and means."[1] " The administration of each society is exercised in so remote spheres that they can never possibly meet to clash, and those societies which never clash, necessity of State can never bring into dependency on one another."[2] Further, " having found that each society is sovereign and independent of the other, it as necessarily follows that . . . union can be produced only by free convention and mutual compact."[3]

In reply to the objection that the two societies

[1] *Alliance Between Church and State*, p. 53.
[2] *Ibid.*, p. 40.   [3] *Ibid.*, p. 43.

of Church and State are composed of the same people and, therefore, can no more make a compact with each other than one man can do so with himself, Warburton put forward the theory of corporate personality. "If two societies have really two distinct wills and two distinct personalities, the subject matter of which these two artificial bodies are composed being one and the same (namely natural bodies specifically and numerically the same) cannot possibly hinder those two societies from entering into compact, and from that compact's having the effects of such as are adjudged most real. That two such societies have two distinct wills and personalities, I shall show. When any number of men form themselves into a political society, whether civil or religious, that society becomes a body different from what the number of individuals made before the society was formed. Otherwise, the society is nothing, or in other words no society is formed. Here is then a body distinct from what the number of individuals make . . . it is the creature of human will. But a body must have its proper personality and will, which without those is a name, a shadow and no more . . . We conclude then that the will and personality of a community is as different and distinct from the will and personality of the individuals of which it is composed as the body itself is."[1] Hence, a number of men can make any number of societies according to the numbers of their wants or ends towards which societies are directed. Among these the Church is one, and "the Church

[1] *Alliance Between Church and State*, pp. 101–102.

being a real society (no argument being brought against that reality but what holds equally against the State's) must have her *distinct* rights,"[1] distinct, that is to say, previous to her entry upon an artificial compact, on the terms of which some of these rights were surrendered for a period just so long as the compact remained unrescinded by either side.

In all this Warburton was but developing a stage further the theory of Church-State relationship, elaborated by Leslie a quarter of a century before. Leslie's federal (but never incorporating) union wherein the two " can never clash more than two parallel lines can meet, because they act in different spheres,"[2] became under Warburton's hand the alliance of two corporate personalities which form a " politic league for mutual support and defence,"[3] and whose administrations are "exercised in so remote spheres that they can never possibly meet to clash." Later, the idea of corporate personalities was to develop into the conception of the Church as a *societas perfecta*, by which doubt was to be cast on the advisability—the possibility, even—of continuing any recognizable or definite association with the State. Such association necessarily demanded the resignation of a measure of autonomy on the part of the Church. Could such a submission, even to a minimum demand of a secular State be found compatible with the high calling of a religious society claiming to be the Body of Christ? The

[1] *Alliance Between Church and State*, p. 106.
[2] Leslie, *Rehearsal*, II, 27.
[3] Warburton, *Alliance*, p. 55.

Tractarians were to come face to face with the same problem, but before it became urgent in their time, speculation on the status of the Church as an ecclesiastical organization was to be temporarily submerged under two very different waves of thought which flooded English religious life in the latter half of the eighteenth century.

The first of these was the development of the rationalistic habit of mind which grew out of the controversies of earlier years. The Church found herself on the defensive against the doctrinal attack of the Deists, and was forced to concentrate attention on an attempt at rational justification for the faith which she was supposed to incorporate. The reasonableness of Christianity—to use Locke's phrase—was the subject of discussion, primarily with reference to its essential dogmas, and later to the evidence on which they were based. There was but little energy left over from this debate, and from the effort put forward to maintain Christian practices in a corrupt and degraded social environment, wherewith to attempt the solution of the problem of Church-State relationships. Nor, on the other hand, did the second great movement of the age have much bearing on speculative thought regarding the nature of the Church. The spiritual revival, which within the Church was known as Evangelicalism and, outside, grew into the separate sect of Methodism, stressed the individualistic side of religion. It put new life into the conception of religion as an indwelling spirit, and emphasized man's personal and direct relationship with God in such a way that the thought of the Church as a society, having a corporate life and specific connection with other societies, tended to fall into the background.

By the nineteenth century the Church had resigned the intellectual leadership of the nation without even being aware of the fact. She was fulfilling a useful function in the country as a centre of philanthropic and cultural activity, but she neither asked for, nor received, the respect due to a sacred and mystical society, which in theory she purported to be. The task which faced the leaders of the Oxford Movement was to restate the intellectual apologetic for Christianity itself as a counter-attack to the liberal philosophy which either ignored or attempted to refute it. Secondly, they had to revive the influence of the Church, to rescue her from secularizing tendencies and restore her to a position in which she would not only merit veneration as a divine and holy institution, but would once more become the accepted leader of the nation—the same position, in fact, which had been built up for her in the theory of the High Church theologians of the seventeenth century, to whom they confessedly owed so much. It is significant that a new edition of Leslie's *Case of the Regale* was published in 1838, when the influence of the Oxford leaders was at its height. The publisher's advertisement on that occasion explained the relevance of the issue—" the above treatise," it ran, " was published . . . when the principle of the ecclesiastical and civil powers had been thrown into confusion by the Revolution of 1688. Its object is to fix the respective limits of these several authorities and to exhibit the theory of their combined operation in the so-called Union of Church and State. It is hoped that its present republication may serve as an antidote to the opinions which still prevail on this vital question, and at the moment threaten to bring the gravest practical evils upon the Church of England." That Leslie's vision of the two societies each functioning in its own sphere, each offering to and receiving support from the other, yet each essentially independent in its government, had never in fact been perfectly embodied in post-Reformation England, was no sufficient reason that it should not be so embodied in the future. Certainly it was obvious by the nineteenth century that the Church of England could not be made co-extensive with the nation in its membership, but at least the relations between the two societies might be perfected as far as they went. " What he fought for," wrote Dean Church of R. H. Froude, " was not Rome, not even a restoration of unity, but a Church of England such as it was conceived of by the Caroline divines and the Non-jurors."[1] Froude himself, in a sentence remarkably reminiscent of the demand for the proper exercise of Church discipline which Leslie made in his Preface to the *Case of the Regale*,[2] declared that, " if a National Church means a Church without discipline, my argument for discipline is an argument against a National Church ; and the best thing we

[1] *R.W. Church, The Oxford Movement*, p. 51.
[2] Second Edition 1702. The passage is too long to quote. The greater part of pages xv–xxv is occupied with a discussion of the problem. Leslie strongly blames the Clergy for refusing to exercise discipline owing to their fear of the temporal powers.

can do is to unnationalize ours as soon as possible."[1] But to "unnationalize" the Church was, a century ago, a vague threat rather than a considered policy. In any case, it was an expedient for which the great majority of Anglicans were not ready. The Anglo-Catholics had yet to put in many years of arduous spade-work on the ground which the Nonjurors had begun to prepare, before they could create suitable conditions for the growth of their seminal idea of the two independent societies.

The life of the Oxford Movement has been dated by Newman from July 4th, 1833, when Keble preached his celebrated Assize sermon on "National Apostasy." A fortnight later the writing of the *Tracts for the Times*, was being considered by a group of four Oxford men who had met for discussion under a deep concern for the spiritual well-being of the Anglican Church in the face of a growing Liberalism in the thought of the Nation. It was the epoch of Benthamism, and however valuable the utilitarian theory might be as a motive for political reform, it was not calculated as a philosophical principle to inspire any great devotion to the spiritual claims of the Church. After the great political changes epitomized in the repeal of the Test and Corporation Acts, the emancipation of the Roman Catholics, and the 1832 Reform Act, the Government was largely supported by those whose interests were hostile to the Establishment. While the atmosphere was full of the idea of reform, it was not unnatural that the Church should come in for its share of criticism

[1] Quoted by R. W. Church, in *The Oxford Movement*, p. 54.

along with other institutions which had been overtaken by weakness and corruption, if indeed they had not been altogether asleep. The measure for the reduction of the number of Irish bishoprics seemed a challenge to the High Churchmen to immediate action.

But although the Movement followed on years of such portent, and the personalities which led it were so vivid and powerful that attention became concentrated upon it, it was not alone in its attempts to reformulate the doctrine of the Church's spiritual autonomy, and to discover the formula by which to reconstruct the theory of Church-State relationships in terms suitable to contemporary need. It was not even the first indication of that revival of thought which was to preserve, for a period at least, the Establishment. Newman himself admitted that he learned of "the existence of the Church as a substantive body or corporation,"[1] from Dr. Whately, under whose influence he came in Oxford as early as 1822. Whately was as ardent in his anti-Erastian views as any of the later Oxford men, and held fast to the theory of the dual nature of Church and State as separate societies having reciprocal duties. Another work which contributed to the revival of serious consideration on the status of the Establishment was Samuel Taylor Coleridge's essay on *Church and State*, which was published in 1830. Coleridge was not accepted as an authority by the majority of Tractarians, though Charles Marriot owed a good deal to his doctrine of the Church, which doctrine

[1] *Apologia*, p. 12 (Edition, 1890).

Newman discovered, somewhat to his surprise, to have much in common with his own. His influence outside Oxford must not be ignored; it was through his book that Gladstone was first aroused to a sense of the reality and urgency of the ecclesiastical problem,[1] and Gladstone's adherence to High Church principles was a factor of no little significance in nineteenth-century politics. Coleridge, no doubt, helped to focus the minds of thoughtful men on the idea of the Church as a supernatural society, the essential life of which was something far different from the trappings of Establishment and privilege with which it was apt to be clothed, and by which it was not infrequently more hampered than assisted in the performance of its true function.

At the outset of the Movement, Newman devoted Tract No. 1 to an exposition of the doctrine of Apostolic succession. He saw that to regain a vivid sense of the divine authority with which the Clergy were commissioned, was to go far towards regaining a sense of the divine nature of the Church. Addressing his brethren in the Ministry, he wrote : " Should the Government and the country so far forget their God as to cast off the Church, to deprive it of its temporal honours and substance, on what will you rest the claim of respect and attention which you make upon your flocks ? There are some who rest their divine mission on their own unsupported assertion ; others who rest it upon their popularity ; others on their success and others who rest it upon their temporal distinctions. This last case has

[1] Morley, *Life of Gladstone*, I, p. 169.

perhaps been too much our own; I fear we have neglected the real ground upon which our authority is built—OUR APOSTOLICAL DESCENT." A divinely commissioned Ministry is the corollary of a divinely instituted and governed Church. The history of the Church, her origins and early fathers; the dogmas she had taught, the heresies she had repudiated, her message, her sacraments, and her authority—these became the objects of study to all members of the Tractarian Party. To the minds of some thus occupied, the Anglican Church came to appear in the guise of a schismatical communion; these left her to become attached to Rome. To many of those who regarded the Reformation as an incident in the continuous history of the English Church, rather than as an Act of schism, the name Protestant ceased to be a title of honour which it had once been, and became an epithet of abuse. Unless the Anglican Church could claim to be part of the great Catholic and Apostolic Church, she ceased to belong to the Church of Christ on earth. The problem was to reconcile such a claim with her Establishment as part of the Constitution of a secular State.

In his lectures on *The Difficulties of Anglicans*, delivered some five years after he had joined the Church of Rome, and addressed to his former friends who still hesitated to follow him, Newman gave a brilliant analysis of the Tractarian position. The lectures were occasioned by the Privy Council decision in the Gorham case, a case which had caused the attention of the whole of the Established Church to be turned once again to the question of State control, and which became one of the contributory causes of the reconstitution of Convocation for the transaction of business in 1852. Although the conclusions in favour of Romanism at which Newman arrived were unacceptable to the great body of Anglicans, there was much which the remaining members of the Oxford Movement could acknowledge as indisputable truth in his preliminary arguments on the nature of the Church. " What is really meant by a Church," said Newman, " is a religious body which has jurisdiction over its members, or which governs itself ; whereas, according to the doctrine of Erastus, it has no such jurisdiction, really is not a body at all, but is simply governed by the State, and is one department of the State's operations."[1] " Unless the Church has something to say and something to do very different from what the State says and does, Erastianism is the doctrine of common sense."[2] " She [the Church] must have a dogma and Sacraments ; it is a dogma and Sacraments, and nothing else, which can give meaning to a Church or sustain her against the State ; for by these are meant certain facts and acts which are special instruments of spiritual good to those who receive them."[3] " Dogma would be maintained, Sacraments would be administered, religious perfection would be venerated and attempted if the Church were supreme in her spiritual power ; dogma would be sacrificed to expedience, sacraments would be rationalized, perfection would be ridiculed if she was made the slave

---

[1] *The Difficulties of Anglicans*, p. 198.
[2] *Ibid.*, p. 203.   [3] *Ibid.*, p. 214.

of the State. Erastianism then was the one heresy which practically cut at the root of all revealed truth."[1] In this insistence on the Church's spiritual independence as the great essential of her life, Newman was but re-echoing the old High Church doctrine, the reverberations of which had recently been so loud in the Oxford Movement, but which had sounded no less distinctly in the days of Atterbury, Leslie and Kettlewell, and the Caroline divines. " It was," he said, " the first principle of the Movement of 1833, that the Church should have absolute power over her faith, worship and teaching."[2] "The doctrine which it especially opposed was, in ecclesiastical language, the heresy of Erastus, and in political, the Royal Supremacy. The object of its attack was the Establishment considered simply as such."[3]

This far Newman could carry his one-time colleagues with him. Beyond, they could not go. " A National Church ever will be and must be what you have found your own to be—an Erastian body,"[4] he told them. " The Movement, then, and the Establishment were in simple antagonism from the first, although neither Party knew it ; they were logical contradictories . . . what was the life of the one was the death of the other."[5] The simplicity of the alternative which Newman thus set before them has ever been impossible for High Churchmen to accept. They could not then believe that their attacks on th Establishment were necessarily to be destructive

---

[1] *The Difficulties of Anglicans*, p. 102.   [2] *Ibid.*, p. 195
[3] *Ibid.*, p. 101.   [4] *Ibid.*, p. 172.   [5] *Ibid.*, p. 105

they wished for long to be reformers rather than iconoclasts. They refused to admit Newman's conclusion that the only way out of the heresy of Erastianism was the way which led to Rome. To most it appeared that the acceptance of the Pope's jurisdiction would be not liberty for the Church, but only a change of servitude, for Rome would not admit the Anglican Church to her fold on terms any lower than those of incorporation. To embrace the Catholic faith was one thing, and it involved abandoning certain errors in Anglicanism; but to become Roman Catholic was another, for it involved accepting a new set of errors in place of the old.

It needed the protracted controversies over ritualism, which occupied so much of the time and attention of Anglo-Catholics in the late years of the century, to reveal the full extent of illogical absurdity which might be discovered latent in a State-controlled Church. The seemingly endless litigation over the interpretation of the Rubrics did much to awaken the mind of the Church throughout the country to what is yet a third alternative between Popery on the one hand and an ultra-Erastianism on the other. A considerable body of opinion within the Anglican Church now looks towards a severance of her legal connection with the State without thereafter coming under the ægis of Rome, as a possible solution to the perpetual problem of imperfectly adjusted relationship.[1] It is probable that, if and when the time arrives for the Disestablishment of the Church

---

[1] *Cf.* The speeches of the late Bishop Weston of Zanzibar before the Anglo-Catholic Congress and the Lambeth Conference in 1920.

of England, the movement towards its accomplishment will come from within the ranks of the Church.

In a pamphlet issued by the Life and Liberty Movement in 1917, Dr. William Temple expressed the hope "that it may prove possible to win self-government without severing the historic connection between Church and State. It is, of course," he continued, "no honour to the Body and Bride of Christ that the British State should seek alliance with it ; but it is an implied confession of faith on the part of the State which makes opportunities for the permeation of the national life with Christian principle. Consequently, though I would rather see the Church free without establishment, than established without freedom, I cannot advocate Disestablishment if any other way to freedom can be found." The Church of England Assembly (Powers) Act of 1919 (the "Enabling Act"), which was the direct outcome of the Life and Liberty Campaign, was an endeavour to find this other way. By it, "the Church has obtained an Act giving extraordinary powers in regard to legislation touching matters concerning the Church. This is a system of legislation under which a measure escapes that which is the most crucial and important stage of the progress of a Bill in Parliament—namely, the Committee Stage."[1] A measure sent up by the Assembly for the Royal Assent is not subject to amendment by Parliament, but only to a definite acceptance or rejection as it stands. Whether this will provide a degree of autonomy sufficient to ensure

[1] Lord Wrenbury, in *The Times*, November 10th, 1926.

that freedom which is " inherent in the very idea of a Church,"[1] it is as yet too soon to judge. In at least one instance,[2] besides the rejection of the Prayer Book measure in 1927 and 1928, the Parliamentary veto has already been applied. It has yet to be discovered whether the freedom which has so far been achieved can really operate adequately within the limits of the constitution as it now stands. If it be found that in the existing state of affairs the Church is now " established without freedom," there are grounds for presuming that High Churchmen will at last take up the challenge to make it " free without establishment."

If such should prove to be the case, they will be building their free Church on ground which the Nonjurors long ago prepared, on which indeed the foundations were already well marked out more than two centuries ago.

[1] Wm. Temple, *Life and Liberty*, 1917.
[2] The Union of Benefices and Disposal of Churches (Metropolis) measure. November, 1926.

BIBLIOGRAPHY

GENERAL

LORD ACTON, *History of Freedom—Political Thoughts on the Church.*
J. N. FIGGIS, *Churches in the Modern State,* 1914 (2nd ed.); *The Divine Right of Kings,* 1896.
H. J. LASKI, *Political Thought from Locke to Bentham,* 1920; *The Problem of Sovereignty,* 1917.
RICHARD LODGE, *Political History of England,* Vol. VIII, 1896.
LORD MACAULAY, *History of England* (Vols. I, II, III of Edinburgh edition of Life and Works).
F. C. MONTAGUE, *Political History of England,* Vol. VII, 1907.
J. H. OVERTON, *The Non-jurors, Their Lives, Principles and Writings,* 1903.
JOHN STOUGHTON, *History of Religion in England,* 1901 (4th ed.).

CHAPTER I

WILLIAM FALKNER, *Christian Loyalty,* 1679.
ROBERT FILMER, *The Anarchy of a Limited or Mixed Monarchy,* 1679; *The Freeholder's Grand Inquest,* 1679; *The Necessity of the Absolute Power of all Kings,* 1648; *Patriarcha,* 1680.
JAMES I., *An Apology for the Oath of Allegiance,* 1609; *Basilikon Doron,* 1603; *The Duty of a King in His Royal Office,* 1642; *True Law of Free Monarchies,* 1603.
WILLIAM LAUD, *Seven Sermons Preached upon Several Occasions,* 1651.
ROGER MAYNWARING, *Religion and Allegiance,* 1627.
RICHARD MOCKET, *God and the King,* 1615.
JOHN NALSON, *The Common Interest of Kings and People,* 1677.
ROBERT SOUTH, *A Sermon Preached at Lambeth Chapel,* 1661.
ROBERT SYBTHORPE, *Apostolic Obedience,* 1627.

BIBLIOGRAPHY

JOHN TURNER, *A Sermon Preached at Epsom*, 1683.
JAMES USHER, *Two Speeches of the Late Lord Primate Usher*, 1661; *The Power Communicated by God to the Prince*, 1683, (2nd ed., edited by Bishop Sanderson).

CHAPTERS II–VI

JEREMY COLLIER, *The Desertion Discussed*, 1688; *Dr. Sherlock's Case of Allegiance Considered*, 1691; *The History of Passive Obedience*, 1689; *A Persuasive Consideration Tendered to Royalists*, 1695 (2nd ed.); *Vindiciae Juris Regii*, 1689.

SAMUEL GRASCOME, *A Brief Answer to a Late Discourse*, 1691; *Considerations upon the Second Canon*, 1693; *Moderation in Fashion*, 1705; *A Reply to a Vindication of a Discourse*, 1691; *The Resolution of a Case of Conscience*, 1719; *Schism Triumphant*, 1707.

GEORGE HICKES, *An Apology for the New Separation*, 1691; *The Constitution of the Catholic Church*, 1716; *A Discourse of the Sovereign Power* (Sermon before the Artillery Coy.), 1682; *Jovian*, 1683; *Sermon Before the Lord Mayor at Bow*, 1682; *Sermon at Worcester*, 1684.

JOHN KETTLEWELL, *Of Christian Communion*, 1692; *Christianity a Doctrine of the Cross*, 1691; *The Duty of Allegiance*, 1691; *A Letter to Dr. John Tillotson*, 1691; *The Measures of Christian Obedience*, 1681; *The Practical Believer*, 1688; *The Religious Loyalist*, 1685. (All included in Collected Edition, 1719.)

CHARLES LESLIE, *A Battle Royal*, 1711; *The Best Answer ever was Made*, 1709; *Best of All*, 1710 (3rd. ed.); *The Case of the Regale and the Pontificate*, 1702 (2nd. ed); *Cassandra (But I Hope Not)*, 1704; *A Dissertation Concerning Private Judgment*, 1726 (3rd ed.); *The Finishing Stroke*, 1711; *A Letter Concerning the New Separation*, 1719; *The New Association*, 1702 (3rd ed.); *The Rehearsal*, August, 1704, to March, 1708 (O.S.); *The True Notion of the Catholic Church*, 1703; *The Wolf Stripped*, the 2nd Part intituled *The Rights of the Christian Asserted*, 1707.

BIBLIOGRAPHY

WILLIAM SANCROFT, *Modern Policies*, 1653 (4th ed.)
WILLIAM SHERLOCK, *The Case of Allegiance*, 1691 (2nd ed.) ; *The Case of Resistance*, 1684 ; *Sermon at St. Margaret's*, 1685.
JOHN TILLOTSON, *The Lawfulness and Obligation of Oaths*, 1681.
ANON., *A Friendly Conference Concerning the New Oath* . . . 1689.

CHAPTER VII

C. J. ABBEY and J. H. OVERTON, *The English Church in the Eighteenth Century*, 1878.
R. W. CHURCH, *The Oxford Movement*, 1891.
J. A. FROUDE, *The Oxford Counter-Reformation*, 1881 (Short Studies, Vol. V).
JOHN MORLEY, *Life of Gladstone*, 1903.
J. H. NEWMAN, *Difficulties of Anglicans*, 1850 (ed., 1908), *Apologia*, 1864 (ed., 1890)
MARK PATTISON, *Tendencies of Religious Thought in England, 1688–1750* ; (*Essays and Reviews*, 1860.)
HERBERT PAUL, *History of Modern England*, 1904.
EDWARD STILLINGFLEET, *The Case of the Oath of Abjuration Considered*, 1693 ; *Discourse Concerning the Unreasonableness of the New Separation*, 1689 ; *A Vindication of His Majesty's Authority to Fill the Sees*, 1691.
NORMAN SYKES, *Edmund Gibson, Bishop of London, 1669–1748*, 1926.
WILLIAM TEMPLE, *Life and Liberty*, 1917.
WILLIAM WAKE, *Authority of Christian Princes*, 1697.
WILLIAM WARBURTON, *The Alliance Between Church and State*, 1736.
WILFRID WARD, *Life of John Henry, Cardinal Newman*, 1913.

INDEX

ABBOTT, ARCHBISHOP, 17
ACTON, LORD, 105
Advice to his son Henry, 5
Alliance between Church and State, 177–180
Anarchy of a Limited or Mixed Monarchy, 22, 28
ANGLICAN CHURCH, see CHURCH OF ENGLAND
ANGLO - CATHOLIC POLITICAL THEORY, 12–17, 24–33, 160–192
Apologia, 155
Apology for the New Separation, 113
Apology for the Oath of Allegiance, 8, 9
Apostolic Obedience, 14
ATTERBURY, FRANCIS, on ecclesiastical independence, 170–172
AUTHORITY, source and nature, 77–88; and law, 88–92; and the Obedience of the Subject, 92–104; Leslie on, 133–149
Authority of Christian Princes, 171

Basilikon Doron, 3, 4, 9, 10
BANGORIAN CONTROVERSY, 174
BATE'S CASE, 11
Battle Royal, 63
BELLARMINE, CARDINAL, 8
Best Answer, 72, 76, 137
Best of All, 64, 74
BISHOPS, Alliance with James I., 2; trial of, 38; and James II., 39; and the succession, 45; refuse the oaths, 46; of the Nonjuring Church, 54
BREDA, DECLARATION OF, 24

CARTWRIGHT, BISHOP, 49
Case of Allegiance, 59, 80, 85
Case of Resistance, 90, 91, 93
Case of Regale, 150, 153–159, 172, 173, 182, 183
Cassandra, 63, 75
CHARLES I., and Maynwaring, 17; and Scotland, 18
CHARLES II., and liberty of conscience, 24; his death, 35
Christian Communion, Of, 114, 115, 125–127
Christian Loyalty, 23, 28–32
Christianity a doctrine of the Cross, 71, 91, 93, 103
CHURCH, NATURE OF, 149–151, 188; OF ENGLAND, allied to throne, 2, 56; after the Restoration, 24–5; relation to Nonjuring Church, 111–117; and Establishment, 121–130; NONJURING, and Jacobitism, 49; reasons for its existence, 52–55; and schism, 111–117; its decline, 174
CHURCH, DEAN, 183
Church and State, 185
CLARENDON, LORD, 24
COLERIDGE, S. T., 185
COLLIER, JEREMY, on the Establishment, 41; against the Contract, 70; on authority, 86; on law, 92; on non-resistance, 95, 98, 99
Common Interest of Kings and People, 26
COMPTON, BISHOP, 36, 39, 40
CONCESSION THEORY, 71, 104, 147–148

197

INDEX

Constitution of the Catholic Church, 122, 127, 128, 174
CONTRACT THEORY, case against, 66–76
CONVENTION OF 1660, 24; of 1689, 41–46
CONVOCATION, 170–174
Convocation Book, 64
CORONATION OATH, see OATH
CORPORATE PERSONALITY, THEORY OF, 179
COUNCIL OF PEERS, 1688, 44
COURT OF HIGH COMMISSION, 36, 39
COWELL, DR., 11

DECLARATIONS OF INDULGENCE, 37
DEISTS, 156, 181
Desertion Discussed, The, 41, 42
Difficulties of Anglicans, 187–189
Discourse concerning Unreasonableness, 164, 165
Discourse of the Sovereign Power, 67, 68
Dissertation concerning Private Judgment, 149, 153
DIVINE RIGHT. Early seventeenth-century views, 1–18; and Natural Right, 22; and the Church, 35; and Mr. Locke, 73; Leslie on, 133–134, 143; history of the doctrine, 160–162; its survival, 167; OF THE CHURCH, 173
Duty of a King in his Royal office, 4, 6
Duty of Allegiance, 59, 80, 82–85

EPISCOPACY, IN SCOTLAND, 18
EVANGELICAL REVIVAL, 181
EXCLUSION BILL, 27, 36, 57, 66

FALKNER, WILLIAM, on rational foundation of government, 23; political theory of *Christian Loyalty*, 29–32

FILMER, ROBERT, on religious foundation of government, 22; works of, 27–28
Finishing Stroke, 136
FLEMING, CHIEF BARON, on King's prerogative, 11
FRAMPTON, BISHOP, 49
Freeholders' Grand Inquest, 27
Friendly Conference, A, 108–110
FROUDE, R. H., 183

GIBSON, BISHOP, 175–176
GLADSTONE, W. E., 186
God and the King, 10
Good old cause, The, 51
GRASCOME, SAMUEL, on the Nonjurors, 51; on public good, 61; on society, 65; on trusteeship, 87; on public worship, 115; on religion, 118; on the establishment, 125
GUNPOWDER PLOT, 8

HICKES, GEORGE, on Ken, 50; on Exclusion Bills, 57; against the Contract, 66–69; on Sovereignty, 79; on trusteeship, 87; on law, 90; on civil war, 96; on non-resistance, 102; on worship, 115, 116; on Church and State, 122, 127
History of Freedom, 105
History of Passive obedience, 93
HOADLEY, BISHOP, and Leslie, 75; and the Bangorian controversy, 173, 174
HOBBES, THOMAS, on pre-governmental era, 75
HUMBLE PETITION AND ADVICE, 19

"IMMORAL PRAYERS," 48, 106, 111, 116
Interpreter, The, 11, 12

INDEX

JAMES I., and Anglican Church, 1, 2; his political theories, 3–10; reintroduced episcopacy into Scotland, 18
JAMES II., avowal of Roman Catholicism, 25; relation to Anglican Church, 34–40
Jovian, 57, 79, 90, 96, 102

KEBLE, JOHN, 184
KEN, BISHOP, 35, 38, 49
KETTLEWELL, JOHN, on the succession, 59; on aims of government, 62; on the Contract, 70, 71; on authority, 80–86; on law, 91; on non-resistance, 93, 100, 103; on Schism, 114; on worship, 115; on Church and State, 124, 125–127, 130

LAKE, BISHOP, 38, 49
LAUD, ARCHBISHOP, on Church and State, 12, 13, 17
LAW, and authority, 88–92; Leslie on, 135, 136, 140
LAW, WILLIAM, 170, 174
Lawfulness and Obligation of Oaths, 107
LESLIE, CHARLES, on the Nonjurors, 51; on aims of government, 62; on origins, 63–65; on the Contract, 71–76; See also Chap. VI, pp. 131–159, Leslie and Warburton, 180
Letter concerning the New Separation, 165
Letter to a Convocation Man, 171
Letter to Dr. Tillotson, 130
LIFE AND LIBERTY MOVEMENT, 191
LITURGY IN SCOTLAND, 18
LLOYD, BISHOP, 49
LOCKE, WILLIAM, Leslie on his political views, 73–75

MADURA, BISHOP, 36
MAINWARING, ROGER, on the Royal Supremacy, 15; on obedience, 16
Measures of Christian Obedience, 124
MILITIA ACTS, 94
MOCKET, RICHARD, 10
Moderation in Fashion, 51, 118, 125
Modern Policies, 97
MONTAIGNE, BISHOP, 17

NALSON, DR. JOHN, on Divine Right, 26
National Apostasy, 184
NATURAL RIGHTS, influence of doctrine on political theory, 22
New Association, 65; see Chap. VI, pp. 131–159, 165, 167
NEWMAN, J. H., CARDINAL, on democracy, 166; on the Church, 184–190
NONJURING CHURCH, see CHURCH
NON-RESISTANCE, 6, 7, 16, 92–104, 143–145, 173

OATH, of Abjuration, 52, 163; of Allegiance, 8; Coronation, 5, 7; of Supremacy, 8, 94, 123, 155; New oaths of allegiance and Supremacy, 47, 108; see also 107, 163
OVERALL, BISHOP, 64
OXFORD MOVEMENT, 182–190

Patriarcha, 28
Persuasive consideration, 100
POPE, condemns Oath of Allegiance, 8; and the deposing power, 69
POPISH PLOT, 25
Practical Believer, The, 80
PRESBYTERIANISM, and Anglicanism, 18; and the Restoration, 19

INDEX

Preservative against . . . the Nonjurors, 173
PRIMOGENITURE, 57–60

REGENCY SCHEME, 42–45
Rehearsal, 64, 73, 75; see also Chap. VI, pp. 131–159, 180
Religion and Allegiance, 15
Religious Loyalist, 80, 101
Reply to a Vindication, 61, 119
RESTORATION, THE, 19, 20, 66
Rights, Powers, and Privileges of . . . Convocation, 172

SANCROFT, ARCHBISHOP, 35, 36, 38, 39, 40, 44–46; on statesmanship, 97; succeeded by Tillotson, 108; prayers by, 116
Schism Triumphant, 88
SHERLOCK, DR. THOMAS, on the *de facto* King, 59; on law, 90; on non-resistance, 93. See also Kettlewell's arguments against Sherlock's position, pp. 80–86
SOUTH, DR. ROBERT, on religion and the Church, 23
SOVEREIGNTY, see AUTHORITY
STILLINGFLEET, EDWARD, on Nonjuror's position, 53; on Oaths, 164
SYBTHORPE, DR. ROBERT, on Church and State, 14; on obedience, 15

TEMPLE, DR. WILLIAM,, on Church and State, 191, 192
TEST ACTS, 25, 37; proposed repeal of, 177; repeal, 184
THIRTY-NINE ARTICLES, 94
THOMAS, BISHOP, 49
TILLOTSON, DR. JOHN, on oaths, 107, 108
Tracts for the Times, 184, 186
True Law of Free Monarchies, 4–7, 9, 10
True Notion of a Catholic Church, 151
TURNER, BISHOP, 38, 49

UNIFORMITY, ACTS OF, 24, 94

Vindication of His Majesty's Authority, 53
Vindiciae juris Regii, 70, 86, 89, 95, 98, 103

WAKE, BISHOP, 170–172
WARBURTON, BISHOP, 176–180
WESTMINSTER ASSEMBLY, 18
WILLIAM OF ORANGE, invitation to, 38; rejects Regency scheme, 42; calls Council, 44; and the oaths, 108–111; prayers for, 116
WHATELY, DR., 185
WHITE, BISHOP, 38, 49
Wolf Stripped, 64, 151, 153, 159

YORK, DUKE OF, see JAMES II.

For Product Safety Concerns and Information please contact our EU representative GPSR@taylorandfrancis.com
Taylor & Francis Verlag GmbH, Kaufingerstraße 24, 80331 München, Germany

www.ingramcontent.com/pod-product-compliance
Lightning Source LLC
Chambersburg PA
CBHW061446300426
44114CB00014B/1853